Some Eccentrics &

Lewis Melville

Alpha Editions

This edition published in 2023

ISBN : 9789357965927

Design and Setting By
Alpha Editions
www.alphaedis.com
Email - info@alphaedis.com

Contents

NOTE

Of the eight papers printed here, "Some Eighteenth-Century Men About Town," "A Forgotten Satirist: 'Peter Pindar'," "Sterne's Eliza," and "William Beckford, of Fonthill Abbey," have appeared in the *Fortnightly Review*; "Charles James Fox" appeared in the *Monthly Review*, "Exquisites of the Regency" in *Chambers's Journal*, and "The Demoniacs" in the American *Bookman*. To the editors of these periodicals I am indebted either for permission to reprint, or for their courtesy in having permitted me to reserve the right of publication in book form. "Philip, Duke of Wharton" is now printed for the first time.

LEWIS MELVILLE

Some Eighteenth-Century Men about Town

When his Royal Highness George, Prince of Wales, afterwards George IV., freed himself from parental control, and, an ill-disciplined lad, launched himself upon the town, it is well known that he was intimate with Charles James Fox, whom probably he admired more because the King hated the statesman than for any other reason. Doubtless the Prince drank with Fox, and diced with him, and played cards with him, but from his later career it is obvious he can never have touched Fox on that great man's intellectual side; and, after a time, the royal scapegrace, who would rather have reigned in hell than have served in heaven, sought companions to whom he need not in any way feel inferior. With this, possibly sub-conscious, desire, he gathered around him a number of men about town, notorious for their eccentricities and for the irregularity of their lives. With these George felt at home; but, though he was nominally their leader, there can be little doubt that he was greatly influenced by them at the most critical time of a young man's life, to his father's disgust and to the despair of the nation. Of these men the most remarkable were Sir John Lade, George Hanger (afterwards fourth Lord Coleraine of the second creation), and Sir Lumley Skeffington; and, by some chance, it happens that little has been written about them, perhaps because what has been recorded is for the most part hidden in old magazines and newspapers and the neglected memoirs of forgotten worthies. Yet, as showing the temper of the times, it may not be uninteresting to reconstruct their lives, and, as far as the material serves, show them in their habit as they lived.

Sir John Lade, the son of John Inskipp, who assumed the name of Lade, and in whose person the baronetcy that had been in the family was revived, was born in 1759, and at an early age plunged into the fast society of the metropolis with such vigour that he had earned a most unenviable reputation by the time he came of age, on which auspicious occasion, Dr Johnson, who knew him as the ward of Mr Thrale, greeted him savagely in the satirical verses which conclude:

"Wealth, my lad, was made to wander:

Let it wander at its will;

Call the jockey, call the pander,

Bid them come and take their fill.

When the bonnie blade carouses,

Pockets full and spirits high—

What are acres? what are houses?

Only dirt, or wet and dry.

Should the guardian friend or mother

Tell the woes of wilful waste,

Scorn their counsels, scorn their pother,

You can hang, or drown, at last."

Sir John became one of the Prince of Wales's cronies, and for a while had the management of his Royal Highness's racing stable; but while it has been hinted of him, as of George Hanger, that during his tenure of that office he had some share in the transactions that resulted in Sam Chifney, the Prince's jockey, being warned off the turf, it is but fair to state that there is no evidence in existence to justify the suspicion. Indeed, he seems to have been honest, except in incurring tradesmen's debts that he could never hope to discharge; but this was a common practice in fashionable circles towards the end of the eighteenth century, and was held to throw no discredit on the man who did so—for was it not a practice sanctioned by the example of "The First Gentleman of Europe" himself?

Sir John's ambition, apparently, was to imitate a groom in dress and language. It was his pleasure to take the coachman's place, and drive the Prince's "German Waggon,"[1] and six bay horses from the Pavilion at Brighton to the Lewes racecourse; and, in keeping with his *pose*, he was overheard on Egham racecourse to invite a friend to return to dinner in these terms:—"I can give you a trout spotted all over like a coach dog, a fillet of veal as white as alabaster, a 'pantaloon' cutlet, and plenty of pancakes as big as coach-wheels—so help me."

Dr Johnson naturally took an interest in Sir John, and, when Lady Lade consulted him about the training of her son, "Endeavour, madam," said he, "to procure him knowledge, for really ignorance to a rich man is like fat to a sick sheep, it only serves to call the rooks round him." It is easier, however, to advocate the acquisition of knowledge than to inculcate it, and knowledge, except of horses, Sir John Lade never obtained in any degree. Indeed, his folly was placed on record by "Anthony Pasquin" in

AN EPIGRAMMATIC COLLOQUY,
Occasioned by Sir John Lade's Ingenious Method of Managing his Estates.

Said Hope to Wit, with eager looks,

And sorrow streaming eyes:

"In pity, Jester, tell me when,

Will Johnny Lade be—wise?"

"Thy sighs forego," said Wit to Hope,

"And be no longer sad;

Tho' other foplings grow to men,

He'll always be—a *Lad*."

Sir John Lade

When Sir John was little more than a boy, Johnson, half in earnest, proposed him as a fitting mate for the author of "Evelina," so Mrs Thrale states; and, indeed, Miss Burney herself records a conversation in 1778 between that lady and the doctor. The inadvisability of the union, however, soon became apparent, and when Sir John, a little later, asked Johnson if he would advise him to marry, "I would advise no man to marry, sir," replied the great man, "who is not likely to propagate understanding"; but the baronet, who doubtless thought this was an excellent joke, and as such intended, crowned his follies by espousing a woman of more than doubtful character. When Sir John met his future wife, she was a servant at a house of ill-fame in Broad Street, St Giles, and, rightly or wrongly, was credited with having been the mistress of Jack Rann, the highwayman, better known as "Sixteen-string Jack," who deservedly ended his career on the gallows in 1774. Marriage did not apparently mend her manners or her morals, for, according to Huish—who, it must, however, be admitted, was an arrant scandalmonger—she was for some time the mistress of the Duke of York, and also acted as procuress for the Prince of Wales; while her command of bad language was so remarkable that the Prince used to say of any foul-mouthed man: "He speaks like Letty Lade."

Like her husband, Lady Lade was a fine whip, and many stories are told of her prowess as a driver of a four-in-hand.

"More than one steed Letitia's empire feels,

Who sits triumphant o'er the flying wheels;

And, as she guides them through th' admiring throng,

With what an air she smacks the silken thong.

Graceful as John, she moderates the reins;

And whistles sweet her diuretic strains;

Sesostris-like, such charioteers as these

May drive six harness'd princes, if they please."

Lady Lade offered to drive a coach against another tooled by a sister-whip eight miles over Newmarket Heath for five hundred guineas a side, but, when it came to the point, no one had sufficient confidence to take up the wager. There is, however, an account of another race in which she participated: "Lady Lade and Mrs Hodges are to have a curricle race at Newmarket, at the next Spring Meeting, and the horses are now in training. It is to be a five-mile course, and great sport is expected. The construction of the traces is to be on a plan similar to that of which Lord March, now Marquis of Queensberry, won his famous match against time. The odds, at present, are in favour of Lady Lade. She runs a grey mare, which is said to be the best horse in the Baronet's stalls."

Like the rest of his set, Sir John spent his patrimony and fell upon evil days, which ended, in 1814, in imprisonment for debt in the King's Bench, being, as Creevey happily puts it, "reduced to beggary by having kept such good company." Some arrangement was made with his creditors, and Sir John was released; whereupon Lord Anglesea went to the Prince of Wales, and insisted upon his giving Lade five hundred a year out of his Privy Purse—no easy task, one may imagine, for "Prinney" was not given to providing for his old friends. William IV. continued the annuity, but reduced it to three hundred pounds, and it was feared that at his death it would be discontinued. However, when the matter was put before Queen Victoria, she, hearing that Sir John was in his eightieth year, generously expressed the intention to pay the pension, which she put as a charge on her Privy Purse, for the rest of his life. Sir John was thus freed from anxiety, but he did not long enjoy her Majesty's bounty, for he died on 10th February 1838, having outlived his wife by thirteen years.

A more interesting and a more intelligent man was George Hanger, who born in 1751, and, after attending a preparatory school, was sent to Eton and Göttingen, and was gazetted in January 1771, an ensign in the first regiment of Foot Guards. In the army he distinguished himself chiefly by his harum-scarum mode of living, and by his adventures, most of which were of too delicate a nature to bear repetition, though his quaint "Memoirs" throw a light upon the company he kept. He met a beautiful gipsy girl, styled by him "the lovely Ægyptea of Norwood," who, according to his account, had an enchanting voice, a pretty taste for music, and played charmingly on the dulcimer. She won his heart with a song, the refrain of which ran:

"Tom Tinker's my true love,

And I am his dear;

And all the world over,

His budget I'll bear."

He married her according to the rites of the tribe, introduced her to his brother officers, and bragged to them of her love and fidelity; but, alas! the song which enchanted him was based, not upon fiction, but upon fact, and after Hanger had lived in the tents with his inamorata for a couple of weeks, he awoke one morning to learn she had run off with a bandy-legged tinker.

For some years he remained in the Foot Guards, where he was very popular with his brother officers; but in 1776 he threw up his commission in anger at someone being promoted over his head, unjustly, as he thought. His early love of soldiering, however, was not yet abated, and he sought and obtained a captaincy in the Hessian Jäger corps, which had been hired by the British Government to go to America. He was delighted with his new uniform—a short, blue coat with gold frogs, and a very broad sword-belt—and, thus attired, swaggered about the town in great spirits, to the accompaniment of his friends' laughter. During the siege of Charlestown he was aide-de-camp to Sir Henry Clinton; he was wounded in an action at Charlottetown in 1780, and two years later was appointed Major in Tarleton's Light Dragoons, which regiment, however, was disbanded in 1783, when Hanger was given the brevet rank of Colonel, and placed on half pay.

At the close of the war Hanger left America for England, but his affairs were in such an unsettled state that he thought it advisable to go direct to Calais, where he remained until his friend, Richard Tattersall, could arrange his affairs. Hanger attributed his insolvency at this time to the fact that the lawyer to whom he had given a power of attorney having died, his estate was sold for the benefit of the mortgagee at half its value. This is probably true, but it is certainly only a half-truth, for his embarrassment was mainly caused by his extravagance when he was in the Foot Guards. He did not often play cards, but he was passionately fond of the turf, kept a stable at Newmarket, and bet heavily on all occasions, though it is said that on the whole he was a considerable winner, and it is recorded that he won no less than seven thousand pounds on the race between Shark and Leviathan. His pay in the Foot Guards of four shillings a day did not, of course, suffice even for his mess-bills, and he wasted much money on dissipation, and more on his clothes. "I was extremely extravagant in my dress," he admitted. "For one winter's dress-clothes only it cost me nine hundred pounds. I was always handsomely dressed at every birthday; but for one in particular I put myself to a very great expense, having two suits for that day. My morning vestments cost me near eighty pounds, and those for the ball above one hundred and eighty. It was a satin coat *brodé en plain et sur les coutures*, and the first satin coat that had ever made its appearance in this country. Shortly after, satin dress-clothes became common among well-dressed men."2

On his return to England, Hanger stayed with Tattersall for a year, and then was engaged in the recruiting service of the Honourable East India Company at a salary which, with commission, never amounted to less than six hundred pounds a year; and he was also appointed, with a further three hundred pounds a year, an equerry to the Prince of Wales, with whom he was on very intimate terms.

The next few years were the happiest of his life, but misfortune soon overcame him. His employment under the East India Company came to an abrupt end owing to a dispute between the Board of Control and the Company, relative to the building of a barrack in this country to receive the East India recruits prior to embarkation, which ended in a change of the whole system of recruiting, when Hanger's services were no longer required. This was bad enough, but worse was to come, for when he had served as equerry for four years, the Prince of Wales's embarrassed affairs were arranged by Parliament, which, making the essential economies, dismissed Hanger.

When this happened, having no means whatever with which to meet some comparatively trifling debts, he surrendered to the Court of King's Bench, and was imprisoned within the Rules from June 1798 until April in the following year, when the successful issue of a lawsuit enabled him to compound with his creditors. "Twice have I begun the world anew; I trust the present century will be more favourable to me than the past," he wrote in his "Memoirs"; and it is much to his credit that instead of whining and sponging on his friends, having only a capital of forty pounds, he started in the business—he called it the profession—of coal-merchant.

According to Cyrus Redding, who used to meet him at the house of Dr Wolcot ("Peter Pindar"), Hanger had fallen out of favour with the Prince by administering a severe reproof to that personage and to the Duke of York for their use of abominable language, and was no longer invited to Carlton House. This, however, does not ring true, for Hanger's language was none of the choicest, and if there was any disagreement, this can scarcely have been the cause. Indeed, if at this time there was a quarrel, it must soon have been made up; and undoubtedly the twain were on friendly terms long after, for when Hanger was dealing in coal, the Prince, riding on horseback, stopped and made friendly inquiry: "Well, George, how go coals now?" to which Hanger, who had a pretty wit, replied with a twinkle, "Black as ever, please your Royal Highness." Certainly Hanger felt no grievance concerning the alleged quarrel, for in his "Memoirs" he spoke in high terms of the heir-apparent in a passage that deserves to be read, as one of the few sincere tributes ever paid to the merits of that deservedly much-abused person.

Whether through the influence of the Prince of Wales or another, Hanger was in 1806 appointed captain commissary of the Royal Artillery Drivers, from which he was allowed to retire on full pay two years later, a proceeding which drew some observations from the Commissioners of Military Inquiry in their seventeenth report, to which Hanger published an answer. As the years passed, however, the free manners and the coarse outspokenness of the Colonel jarred on the Prince, and slowly the men drifted more and more apart, after which the former moved in less distinguished and probably less vicious company.

The first Lord Coleraine had long since been dead; Hanger's eldest brother, the second Baron, had followed his father to the grave, and the title was now enjoyed by his second brother, William, popularly known as "Blue" Hanger, from the colour of the clothes he wore in his youth. Charles Marsh declared him to be "perhaps the best-dressed man of his age," which is an ambitious claim for any person in the days when clothes were more regarded in fashionable society than anything else in the world; but that there was some ground for the statement cannot be doubted, since "Tom" Raikes reiterates it. "He was a *beau* of the first water, always beautifully powdered, in a light green coat, with a rose in his buttonhole. He had not much wit or talent, but affected the *vieille cour* and the manners of the French Court; he had lived a good deal in Paris before the Revolution, and used always to say that the English were a very good nation, but they positively knew not how to make anything but a kitchen poker. I remember many years ago, the Duchess of York made a party to go by water to

Richmond, in which Coleraine was included. We all met at a given hour at Whitehall Stairs, and found the Admiralty barge, with the Royal Standard, ready to receive us, but by some miscalculation of the tide, it was not possible to embark for near half-an-hour, and one of the watermen said to the Duchess, 'Your Royal Highness must wait for the tide.' Upon which Coleraine, with a very profound bow, remarked, 'If I had been the tide I should have waited for your Royal Highness.' Nothing could have been more stupid, but there was something in the manner in which it was said that made everyone burst out laughing." "Blue" Hanger, it will be seen, was as remarkable for his politeness as for his satire!

Heavy losses at the card-table forced William Hanger to go abroad to avoid his creditors, and he remained in France until the death of his elder brother in 1794, when, able to settle his affairs, he returned, completely transformed in manners and appearance into a Frenchman. Thereby hangs the story that, shortly after he arrived in England, he went to Drury Lane, when, next to him in the dress circle sat a stranger wearing top-boots. This would have been regarded as a gross breach of etiquette in France, and Lord Coleraine was not inclined to brook this affront to the company because he was in England.

"I beg, sir, you will make no apology," he said, with an innocent and reassuring air.

His neighbour stared in blank amazement. "Apology, sir! Apology for what?" he demanded angrily.

"Why," said "Blue," pointing to the offending boots, "that you did not bring your horse with you into the box."

"Perhaps it is lucky for you I did not bring my *horsewhip*," retorted the other, in a fine frenzy of passion; "but I have a remedy at hand, and I will pull your nose for your impertinence." Whereupon he threw himself upon Lord Coleraine, only to be dragged away by persons sitting on the other side of him.

Cards were exchanged between the combatants, and a duel seemed imminent. "Blue" went at once to his brother to beg his assistance. "I acknowledge I was the first aggressor," he said, in anything but a humble frame of mind; "but it was too bad to threaten to pull my nose. What had I better do?" To which the unfeeling Colonel made reply, "*Soap it well*, and then it will easily slip through his fingers!"

This characteristic advice George Hanger was never weary of repeating, and he insisted that when anyone wished to calumniate another gentleman, he ought to be careful to take the precaution to *soap his nose* first. "Since I have taken upon myself the charge of my own sacred person," he said, returning to the subject in his "Memoirs," "I never have been pulled by the nose, or been compelled to soap it. Many gentlemen of distinguished rank in this country are indebted to the protecting qualities of soap for the present enjoyment of their noses, it being as difficult to hold a soaped nose between the fingers as it is for a countryman, at a country wake, to catch a pig turned out with his tail soaped and shaved for the amusement of the spectators."

"Blue" Hanger died on 11th December 1814, when the title and estates devolved upon the Colonel, who, however, could never be persuaded to change his name. "Plain George Hanger, sir, if you please," he would say to those who addressed him in the more formal manner. It has generally been supposed that this was merely another of the peer's many eccentricities, but there was a kindly reason for it. "Among the few nobility already named," wrote Westmacott in the long-forgotten "Fitzalleyne of Berkeley," "more than one raised modest birth and merit to their own rank; one made a marriage of reparation; nay, even the lord rat-catcher,3 life-writer (and it was his own), and vendor of the black article of trade, was faithful to his engagements where the law bound him not; and one of his reasons for forbidding his servants to address him as 'My Lord' was that she might bear his name as Mrs Hanger."

Hanger, now in the possession of a competence, made little change in his manner of living, and though death did not claim him until 31st March 1824, at the age of seventy-three, he never again went into general society. At the time of his succession to the peerage he was residing, and during the last years of his life he continued to reside, at Somers Town, whence he would occasionally wander, shillelagh in hand, to the "Sol Arms," in Tottenham Court Road, to smoke a pipe. This has been so often repeated, to the exclusion of almost any other particulars of his life, that the comparatively few people who have heard of Hanger think of him as a public-house loafer; but this was far from being the case, for if he went sometimes to the "Sol Arms" he would also go to Dr Wolcot to converse with the veteran satirist, or to Nollekens, the sculptor; or he would ride on his grey pony so far as Budd & Calkin's, the booksellers in Pall Mall, where, leaving his horse in charge of a boy—for he never took a groom with him—he would sit on the counter, talking with the shopkeepers and their customers.

Nor was Hanger illiterate, as were so many of the associates of his early years, and he wrote very readable letters; but his intelligence does not rest only on his correspondence, for he was an industrious writer on military subjects. Reference has already been made to his autobiography, which appeared in 1801 under the title of "The Life, Adventures, and Opinions of Colonel George Hanger"; but though it was stated on the title-page that the volumes were "Written by Himself," it has since transpired that they were compiled from his papers and suggestions by William Combe, the author of "The Tours of Dr Syntax." It is an unpleasant work, and deals frankly with subjects tacitly avoided by present-day writers; but it is not without value, for it contains, besides excellent descriptions of debtors' prisons and the rogueries of attorneys at the end of the eighteenth century, common-sense views on social subjects—views much in advance of the general opinions of the day—and a frank avowal of hatred of hypocrisy. This last quality induced Hanger maliciously to relate a story of a dissenter who kept a huxter's shop, where a great variety of articles were sold, and was heard to say to his shopman, "John, have you watered the rum?" "Yes." "Have you sanded the brown sugar?" "Yes." "Have you wetted the tobacco?" "Yes." "Then come in to prayers." The "Memoirs" will perhaps best be remembered for Hanger's famous prophecy that "one of these days the northern and southern Powers [of the United States] will fight as vigorously against each other as they have both united to do against the British."

It is, however, not as a soldier, a pamphleteer, or a seer that Hanger has come down to posterity; and while some may recall that in 1772 he distinguished himself by being one of the gentlemen who, with drawn swords, forced a passage for the entry of Mrs Baddeley into the Pantheon, and eight and thirty years later rode on his grey palfrey in the procession formed in honour of the release of Sir Francis Burdett, it is for his eccentricities and his humour that he is remembered. Nollekens has related how one day he overheard Lord Coleraine inquire of the old apple-woman at the corner of Portland Road, evidently an old acquaintance, who was packing up her fruit, "What are you about, mother?" "Why, my Lord, I am going home to tea." "Oh! don't baulk trade. Leave your things on the table as they are; I will mind shop till you return"; and the peer seated himself in the old woman's wooden chair, and waited until the meal was over, when he solemnly handed her his takings, threepence halfpenny.

Although Cyrus Redding declared that Hanger was well known in his day for an original humour which spared neither friend nor foe, and although Hanger could sneer at those who accepted the invitations to dinner that Pitt was in the habit of sending to refractory members of his party—"The rat-trap is set again," he would say when he heard of such dinner-parties: "is the bait *plaice* or paper?"—there were many who found themselves in a position to praise Hanger's generosity. We have it on the authority of Westmacott—and there can be no surer tribute than this, since Westmacott would far rather have said a cruel than a kind thing—that Hanger never forgot a friend or ignored an acquaintance because he had fallen upon evil days. When an out-at-elbows baronet came to see him, Hanger received him heartily, insisted upon his remaining as his guest for some time, and, summoning his servants, addressed them characteristically: "Behold this man, ye varlets! Never mind me while he is here; neglect me if ye will, but look upon him as your master; obey him in all things; the house, the grounds, the game, the gardens, all are at his command; let his will be done; make him but welcome, and I care not for the rest." For his kind heart much may be forgiven Hanger; and who could be angry with a man who possessed so keen a sense of humour as is revealed in this story? Late one night he went into his bedroom at an inn, and found it occupied. The opening of the door awoke an irate Irishman, the occupier, who inquired in no measured terms: "What the devil do you want here, sir? I shall have satisfaction for the affront. My name is Johnson." Aroused by the clamour, a wizen-faced woman by Johnson's side raised her head from the pillow. "Mrs Johnson, I presume?" said Hanger dryly, bowing to the lady.

Sir Lumley St George Skeffington had at least more claim to distinction than most of his brother fops, though it was their habit to sneer at him, especially after Byron had given them the cue. Born on 23rd March 1771, Lumley was educated at Henry Newcome's school at Hackney, where he showed some taste for composition and poetry, and took part in the dramatic performances for which that institution had been noted for above a century. On one occasion there he delivered an epilogue written by George Keate, the subject of which was the folly of vanity; but the lad did not take the lesson to heart, for so soon as he was his own master he set up as a leader of fashion. At an early age he began to be talked about, and such notoriety was the *open sesame* to Carlton House. The Prince of Wales condescended to discuss costume with the young man, who, thus encouraged, was spurred to fresh efforts, and acquired fame as the inventor of a new colour, known during his lifetime as Skeffington brown. Indeed, Skeffington, who was vain of his personal appearance—though, it must be confessed, without much reason—dressed in the most foppish manner; and as an example may be given a description of his costume at the Court held in honour of the King's birthday in 1794: "A brown spotted silk coat and breeches, with a white silk waistcoat richly embroidered with silver, stones, and shades of silk; the design was large baskets of silver and stones, filled with bouquets of roses, jonquilles, etc., the *ensemble* producing a beautiful and splendid effect."

Though elated at being recognised as a *beau*, Skeffington did not desert his first love, and he mixed much in theatrical society, and became on intimate terms with many of the leading actors, including Joseph Munden, John Kemble, Mrs Siddons, and T. P. Cooke. He was an inveterate "first-nighter," and would flit from theatre to theatre during the evening; but he was not content to be a hanger-on to the fringe of the dramatic profession, and desired to be a prominent member of the *coterie*. He had abandoned any idea of following up his youthful successes as an actor, but he had so early as 1792, at the age of one and twenty, made his bow as an author, with a prologue to James Plumptre's comedy, *The Coventry Act*, performed at the latter's private theatre at Norwich.

Spurred by the praise bestowed upon this trifle, he penned complimentary verses to pretty actresses; but after a time he aspired to greater distinction, and endeavoured to secure literary laurels by the composition of several plays. His *Word of Honour*, a comedy in five acts, was produced at Covent Garden Theatre in 1802, and in the following year his *High Road to Marriage* was staged at Drury Lane; but neither of these had any sort of success, and it was not until *The Sleeping Beauty* was performed at Drury Lane, in December 1805, that the author could look upon his efforts with any pride.

To judge from a contemporary account, *The Sleeping Beauty*, with music by Addison, was an agreeable, albeit an over-rated, entertainment of the nature of an extravaganza. "Mr Skeffington," we are told, "has not confined himself to the track of probability; but, giving the rein to his imagination, has boldly ventured into the boundless region of necromancy and fairy adventure. The valorous days of Chivalry are brought to our recollection, and the tales which warmed the breasts of youth with martial ardour are again rendered agreeable to the mind that is not so fastidious as to turn with fancied superiority from the pleasing delusion. The ladies in particular would be accused of ingratitude were they to look coldly upon the Muse of Mr Skeffington, who had put into the mouths of his two enamoured knights speeches and panegyrics upon the sex, which would not discredit the effusions of Oroondates, or any other hero of romance."

The book of the play was never printed, but the song, duets, and choruses of this "grand legendary melodrama" were published, and so it is possible to form some opinion of the merits of this production of the author, who is described by a writer in *The Gentleman's Magazine* as "the celebrated Mr Skeffington . . . a gentleman of classic genius, [who] it is well known figures high in the most fashionable circles." It is to be feared that Skeffington's fame as a man of fashion threw a glamour upon this critic, for to modern eyes the "classic genius" is nowhere in evidence, although the verses certainly do not compare unfavourably with the drivel offered by the so-called lyric writers whose effusions figure in the musical comedies of to-day.

Unexpectedly, however, *The Sleeping Beauty* achieved immortality, though not an immortality of the pleasantest kind, for the piece attracted the attention of Byron, who pilloried it in his "English Bards and Scotch Reviewers":

"In grim array though Lewis' spectres rise,

Still Skeffington and Goose4 divide the prize:

And sure great Skeffington must claim our praise,

For skirtless coats and skeletons of plays,

Renown'd alike; whose genius ne'er confines

Her flight to garnish Greenwood's gay designs;

Nor sleeps with 'sleeping beauties,' but anon

In five facetious acts come thundering on,

While poor John Bull, bewilder'd with the scene,

Stares, wond'ring what the devil it can mean;

But as some hands applaud—a venal few—

Rather than sleep, John Bull applauds it too."

For years before this satire appeared Skeffington was a personage in society, and if his plays secured him undying notoriety at the hands of the satirist, his costume was to produce the same result by the attention drawn to it by Gillray, who represented him, in 1799, as "Half Natural," in a Jean de Bry coat, all sleeves and padding, and in the following year in a second caricature as dancing, below which is the legend: "So Skiffy skipt on, with his wonted grace." In these days, indeed, his appearance offered a very distinct mark for the caricaturist. Imagine a tall, spare man, with large features, sharp, sallow face, and dark curly hair and whiskers, arrayed in the glory of a dark blue coat with gilt buttons, yellow waistcoat, with cord inexpressibles, large bunches of white ribbons at the knees, and short top-boots! But in latter years Skeffington went even further, for he distinguished himself by wearing a *vieux-rose* satin suit, and a wig, and rouging his cheeks and blacking his eyebrows and eyelashes, until he looked like a French doll; while the air in his vicinity was made noxious by the strong perfumes with which he drenched himself. Horace Smith summed him up as "an admirable specimen of the florid Gothic," and Moore lampooned him in Letter VIII. of *The Twopenny Post Bag*, from "Colonel Th-m-s to Sk-ff-ngt-n, Esq.":

"Come to our *fête*, and bring with thee

Thy newest best embroidery,

Come to our *fête*, and show again

That pea-green coat, thou pink of men,

Which charmed all eyes that last surveyed it;

When Brummell's self enquired: 'Who made it?'

Oh! come (if haply 'tis thy week

For looking pale) with paly cheek;

Though more we love thy roseate days,

When the rich rouge pot pours its blaze

Full o'er thy face, and amply spread,

Tips even thy whisker-tops with red—

Like the last tints of dying day

That o'er some darkling grove delay.

Put all thy wardrobe's glories on,

And yield in frogs and fringe to none

But the great Regent's self alone."

Skeffington's success with *The Sleeping Beauty* occurred at the time when he was most prominent in society. "I have had a long and very pleasant walk to-day with Mr Ilingworth in Kensington Gardens, and saw all the extreme crowd there about three o'clock, and between that and four," Lord Kenyon wrote to his wife on 1st June 1806. "The most conspicuous figure was Mr Skeffington, with Miss Duncan leaning on his arm. He is so great an author that all which is done is thought correct, and not open to scandal. To be sure, they looked rather a comical pair, she with only a cap on, and he with his curious whiskers and sharp, sallow face."

Gradually, however, as time changed, Skeffington was left behind in the race, and was no longer regarded as a leader of fashion, and at the same time he was not fortunate enough to win further success as a dramatist, for his *Mysterious Bride* in 1808, his *Bombastes Furioso* played at the Haymarket in 1810, and his *Lose no Time*, performed three years later at Drury Lane, were each and all dire failures.

In January 1815 Sir William Skeffington died, and Lumley succeeded to the baronetcy. Sir William, however, had embarrassed his estates, and Lumley, to save his father from distress, had generously consented to cut the entail, and so had deprived himself of a considerable fortune. The comparatively small amount of money that now came to him had been forestalled, and he was compelled to seek refuge for several years within the rules of the King's Bench Prison. Eventually, though he failed in the attempt to regain an interest in the estates of his maternal family, the Hubbards, at

Rotherhithe, he came into possession of an estate worth about eight hundred pounds a year; but when he came again upon the town his old friends showed a marked disposition to avoid him; and when one day Alvanley was asked who was that solitary, magnificently attired person, "It is a second edition of *The Sleeping Beauty*," he replied wittily; "bound in calf, richly gilt, and illustrated by many cuts."

Skeffington now resided quietly in Southwark, where he still entertained members of the theatrical profession, but no longer the leaders of the calling, only the members of the adjacent Surrey Theatre. Henry Vizetelly met him towards the end of his life, and described him as "a quiet, courteous, aristocratic-looking old gentleman, an ancient fop who affected the fashions of a past generation, and wore false hair and rouged his cheeks," who had, he might have added, a large fund of *histoires divertissants* with which to regale his visitors.

He outlived all his brother dandies, but to the end would wander in the fashionable streets, recalling the glories of his early manhood, attracting attention in his long-waisted coat, the skirts of which descended to his heels, but recognised by none of the generation that had succeeded his own. In other circles, however, he found listeners interested in his stories of the palmy days of Carlton House, when he was one of the leaders of fashion in society and prominent in the *coulisses*. He died, unmarried, in his eightieth year, and attributed his long life to the fact that he did not stir out of doors in the cold, damp winter months, but moved from room to room so as never to remain in vitiated air.

In conclusion it must be pointed out that Skeffington's popularity was largely contributed to by his good humour and vivacity, and by the fact that in an age when wit spared nobody he was never known to say an unkind word of anyone; nor was the reason for this, as was said of another *beau*, that he never spoke of anyone but himself. "As to his manners, the suffrages of the most polished circles of this kingdom have pronounced him one of the best bred men of the present times, blending at once the decorum of what is called the *vieille cour* with the careless gracefulness of the modern school; he seems to do everything by chance, but it is such a chance as study could not improve," so ran a character sketch of the dandy in *The Monthly Review* for 1806. "In short, whenever he trifles it is with elegance, and whenever occasion calls for energy he is warm, spirited, animated." He had, however, his share of the *nonchalance* affected by the fashionable folk of his day, and the story is told that when, on a visit to a gentleman in Leicester, he was disturbed in the night with the information that the adjoining house was in flames, his sole comment was that this was "a great bore"; and when with difficulty he had been induced to move quickly enough to escape into the street, there, standing in his nightdress, bareheaded and with his hair in papers, he called out, "What are these horrid creatures about with so much filthy water, that I cannot step without wetting my slippers?"

Some Exquisites of the Regency

When Almack's Club, composed of all the travelled young men who wore long curls and spying-glasses, was in 1778 absorbed by Brooks's, the day of the Macaronis was past. Then, as Wraxall records, Charles James Fox and his friends, who might be said to lead the Town, affecting a style of neglect about their persons and manifesting a contempt of all the usages hitherto established, first threw a sort of discredit on dress. "Fox lodged in St James's Street, and as soon as he rose, which was very late, had a *levée* of his followers and of the members of the gambling club at Brooks's—all his disciples," Walpole wrote. "His bristly black person, and shagged breast quite open and rarely purified by any ablutions, was wrapped in a foul linen nightgown, and his bushy hair dishevelled. In these cynic weeds, and with epicurean good humour, did he dictate his politics, and in this school did the heir of the Crown attend his lessons and imbibe them."

The young Prince of Wales might study statecraft under Fox; but in the matter of dress he fell in line with the new race of *beaux*, bucks, or, to use a word that came into general use at this time, dandies. The most famous of the latter were Lord Petersham, Lord Foley, Lord Hertford (immortalised by Thackeray in "Vanity Fair" as the Marquis of Steyne, and by Disraeli in "Coningsby" as Lord Monmouth), the Duke of Argyll, Lord Worcester, Henry Pierrepoint, Henry de Ros, Colonel Dawson Darner, Daniel Mackinnon, Lord Dudley and Ward, Hervey Ashton, Gronow the memoirist, Sir Lumley Skeffington, and Brummell.

These exquisites were disinclined to yield the palm even to an heir-apparent with limitless resources. The Prince of Wales, however, contrived to hold his own. At his first appearance in society he created a sensation. He wore a new shoe-buckle! This was his own invention, and differed from all previous articles of the same kind, insomuch as it was an inch long and five inches broad, reaching almost to the ground on either side of the foot! This was good for an introduction to the polite world, but it was not until he attended his first Court ball that he did himself full justice. Then his magnificence was such that the arbiters of fashion were compelled reluctantly to admit that a powerful rival had come upon the scene. A contemporary was so powerfully impressed by the splendour of the Prince's costume that he placed on record a description: "His coat was pink silk, with white cuffs; his waistcoat white silk, embroidered with various coloured foil, and adorned with a profusion of French paste; and his hat was ornamented with two rows of steel beads, five thousand in number, with a button and loop of the same metal, and cocked in a new military style."

George, Prince of Wales

The laurels won in early youth he retained all the days of his life. Expense was no object to him, and, indeed, it must be confessed he spent money in many worse ways than on his clothes. Batchelor, his valet, who entered his service after the death of the Duke of York, said that a plain coat, from its repeated alterations and the consequent journeys from London to Windsor to Davison the tailor, would often cost three hundred pounds before it met with his approbation! George had a mania for hoarding, and at his death all the coats, vests, breeches, boots, and other articles of attire which had graced his person during half-a-century were found in his wardrobe. It is said he carried the catalogue in his head, and could call for any costume he had ever worn. His executors, Lord Gifford and Sir William Knighton, discovered in the pockets of his coats, besides innumerable women's love letters, locks of hair, and other trifles of his usually discreditable amours, no less than five hundred pocket-books, each containing small forgotten sums of money, amounting in all to ten thousand pounds! His clothes sold for fifteen thousand pounds; they cost probably ten times that amount.

Lord Petersham was a Mæcenas among the tailors, and the inventor of an overcoat called after him. He was famous for his brown carriages, horses, and liveries, all of the same shade; and his devotion to this colour was popularly supposed to be due to the love he had borne a widow of the name. He never went out before six o'clock in the evening, and had many other eccentricities. Gronow has described a visit to his apartments: "The room into which we were ushered was more like a shop than a gentleman's sitting-room. All around the wall were shelves, upon which were placed the canisters containing congou, pekoe, souchong, bohea, gunpowder, Russian, and many other teas, all the best of their kind; on the other side of the room were beautiful jars, with names in gilt letters of innumerable kinds of snuff, and all the necessary apparatus for moistening and mixing. Lord Petersham's mixture is still well known to all tobacconists. Other shelves and many of the tables were covered with a great number of magnificent snuff-boxes; for Lord Petersham had perhaps the finest collection in England, and was supposed to have a fresh box for every day in the year. I heard him, on the occasion of a delightful old light-blue Sèvres box he was using being admired, say in his lisping way, 'Yes, it is a nice summer box, but it would not do for winter wear.'" Queen Charlotte had made snuff-taking fashionable in England, but the habit began to die out with the Regency. George IV. carried a box, but he had no liking for it; and, conveying it with a grand air between his right thumb and forefinger, he was careful to drop it before it reached his nose. He gave up the custom of offering a pinch to his neighbours, and it was recognised as a breach of good manners to dip uninvited into a man's box. When at the Pavilion the Bishop of Winchester committed such an infringement of etiquette, Brummell told a servant to throw the rest of the snuff into the fire. When Lord Petersham died, his snuff was sold by auction. It took three men three days to weigh it, and realised three thousand pounds.

Another eccentric was Lord Dudley and Ward, sometime Secretary of State for Foreign Affairs, who eventually lost his reason. His absence of mind was notorious, and he had a habit of talking aloud that frequently landed him in trouble. Dining at the house of a *gourmet*, under the impression he was at home, he apologised for the badness of the *entrées*, and begged the company to excuse them on account of the illness of his cook! Similarly, when he was paying a visit he imagined himself to be the entertainer, and when his hostess had exhausted her hints concerning the duration of his call, he murmured, "A very pretty woman. But she stays a devilish long time. I wish she'd go." Still more amusing were his remarks in the carriage of a brother peer who had volunteered to drive him from the House of Lords to Dudley House: "A deuce of a bore! This tiresome man has taken me home, and will expect me to ask him to dinner. I suppose I must do so, but it is a horrid nuisance." This was too much for his good-natured companion, who, as if to himself, droned in the same monotonous tones, "What a bore! This good-natured fellow Dudley will think himself obliged to invite me to dinner, and I shall be forced to go. I hope he won't ask me, for he gives d——d bad dinners." These stories recall another related of an absent-minded royal duke, who, when during the service the parson proposed the prayer for rain, said in a voice audible throughout the church, "Yes, by all means let us pray, but it won't be any good. We sha'n't get rain till the moon changes."

After Brummell left England, it was to William, Lord Alvanley that all the witty sayings of the day were attributed. The son of the famous lawyer Sir Pepper Arden,5 he began life in the Coldstream Guards, of which the colonel was the Duke of York. He achieved his earliest success as a wit at the expense of a brother officer, Gunter, a scion of the famous catering-house. Gunter's horse was almost beyond the control of the rider, who explained that his horse was too hot to hold. "Ice him, Gunter; ice him," cried Alvanley. Thrown into such company, it was not perhaps unnatural that Alvanley should be extravagant; but his carelessness in money matters was notorious. He never paid ready money for anything, and never knew the extent of his indebtedness. He had no sympathy with those who devoted some time and trouble to the management of their affairs, and expressed the utmost contempt for a friend who was so weak as to "muddle away his fortune paying tradesmen's bills." Though very wealthy, he soon became embarrassed in his circumstances. He persuaded Charles Greville, the author of the "Journals," to put his affairs in order. The two men spent a day over accounts, and Greville found that the task he had undertaken would not be so difficult as he had been given to understand. His relief was not long-lived, however, for on the following morning he received a note from Alvanley saying he had quite forgotten a debt of fifty thousand pounds!

Alvanley was famous for his dinners, and indulged in the expensive taste of having an apricot tart on his table every day throughout the year. His dinners were generally acclaimed as the best in England; certainly he spared no expense in the endeavour to secure the blue ribbon of the table. Even Abraham Hayward commented on his extravagance. "He had his *suprême de volaille* made of the oysters, or *les sots, les-laissent* of fowls, instead of the fillet from the breast," he noted in "The Art of Dining," "so that it took a score of birds to complete a moderate dish." It was Alvanley who organised a wonderful freak dinner at White's Club, at which the inventor of the most costly dish should dine at the cost of the others; and he won easily. His contribution to the feast was a *fricassée* made of the *noix*, or small pieces at each side of the back, taken from thirteen different kinds of birds, among them being a hundred snipe, forty woodcocks, twenty pheasants—in all some three hundred birds. The cost of this dish exceeded one hundred pounds.

As he was beloved by his friends and vastly popular, society was enraged when O'Connell in the House of Commons spoke of him as "a bloated buffoon." A challenge was sent at once, but the Liberator refused to go out. He had been on the ground once, had killed his man, and had vowed never to fight another duel. Alvanley would not forgive the insult, however, and threatened to thrash the aggressor; whereupon Morgan O'Connell met him in place of his father, when several shots were exchanged without result. "What a clumsy fellow O'Connell must be, to miss such a fat fellow as I!" said Alvanley calmly. "He ought to practise at a haystack to get his hand in." Driven back to London, he gave the hackney-coachman a sovereign. "It's a great deal," said the man gratefully, "for having taken your lordship to Wimbledon." "No, my good fellow," the peer laughed; "I give it you, not for taking me, but for bringing me back."

Beyond all question the greatest dandy of his day was George Bryan Brummell, generally called Beau Brummell. This famous personage dominated all his rivals, and even the Prince of Wales accepted him at least as an equal. It is not known with any certainty how his acquaintance began with the heir-apparent. Brummell's aunt, Mrs Searle, who had a little cottage with stables for cows at the entrance, opposite Clarges Street, of the Green Park, in which she had been installed by George III., related that it was one day when the Prince of Wales, accompanied by the beautiful Marchioness of Salisbury, stopped to see the cows milked that he first met her nephew, was attracted by him, and, hearing he was intended for the army, offered him a commission in his own regiment. Gronow gives another story, which on the face of it is more probable. Brummell made many friends among the scions of good family while he was at Eton, where he seems to have been regarded as an Admirable Crichton: "the best scholar, the best boatman, the best cricketer." He was invited to a ball at Devonshire House, became a great favourite, and was asked everywhere. The Prince sent for him, and, pleased by his manner and appearance, gave him a commission. In his seventeenth year he was gazetted to a cornetcy in the Tenth Light Dragoons. He resigned soon after because the regiment was ordered to Manchester!6

Brummell threw himself heart and soul into the social life of the metropolis, and soon his reputation extended far and wide, until no party was complete without him, and his presence was regarded as the hall-mark of fashion. He was the very man for the part he had set himself. Tall, well made, with a good figure, he affected an old-world air of courtesy, picked up probably from the French refugees, as he had never been out of England until he left it for good. His affectation of *vieille cour* showed itself in the use of powder, which distinguished him in the days when the custom was dying out among civilians. His grandfather was a tradesman, and let lodgings in Bury Street, St James's. His father, by the influence of a lodger, was presented to a clerkship in the Treasury, became private secretary to Lord North, made money by speculation, settled down at Donnington, and became High Sheriff of Berkshire, where he was visited by Fox and Sheridan. Though of no rank, Brummell lived with the highest in the land on terms of equality. His acquaintance was sought, his intimacy desired;

and, so far from requiring a patron, it was he who patronised. His influence was unbounded, his fascination undeniable, his indifference to public opinion reckless. He was good-natured and rarely out of humour; neither a drunkard nor a profligate. He had bright and amusing conversation, some wit, and a considerable power of *persiflage*, which, while it enabled him to laugh some people out of bad habits, only too frequently was exerted to laugh others out of good principles.

He revived the taste for dress. "Clean linen, and plenty of it" was an important item of his creed. His great triumph was in connection with the cravat. Before he came into his own they were worn without stiffening of any kind; as soon as he ascended his throne he had them starched!7 A revolution would not have attracted more attention. Thereafter his sway was undisputed, and his word law in all matters of fashion. The Prince of Wales used to call on him in the morning at his house in Chesterfield Street, and, deeply engrossed in the discussion of costume, would frequently remain to dinner. "Brummell was always studiously and remarkably well dressed, never *outré*; and, though considerable time and attention were devoted to his toilet, it never, when once accomplished, seemed to occupy his attention," said one who knew him well. "His manners were easy, polished, and gentleman-like, and regulated by that same good taste which he displayed in most things. No one was a more keen observer of vulgarity in others, or more *piquant* in his criticisms, or more despotic as an *arbiter elegantarium*; he could decide the fate of a young man just launched into the world with a single word."8

The tastes of the Prince of Wales verged on the florid, but Brummell's efforts tended to simplicity of costume. Under Brummell the dandy's dress consisted of a blue coat with brass buttons, leather breeches, and top-boots; with, of course, the deep, stiff white cravat which prevented you from seeing your boots while standing. Gronow relates that while he was in Paris after Waterloo trousers and shoes were worn by young men, only old fogies favouring knee-breeches. On his return to England in 1816, receiving from Lady Hertford an invitation to Manchester House "to have the honour of meeting the Prince Regent," he went dressed *à la Française*—white neckcloth, waistcoat, black trousers, shoes and silk stockings. He made his bow, and almost immediately afterwards Horace Seymour came to him: "The great man is very much surprised that you should have ventured to appear in his presence without knee-breeches. He considers it as a want of proper respect for him." Gronow went away in high dudgeon. A month later the Prince adopted the dress he had censured!

All the world watched Brummell to imitate him. He made the fortune of his tailor, Weston, of Old Bond Street, and of his other tradesmen. The most noteworthy of these was Hoby, the St James's Street bootmaker, an impertinent and independent man who employed his leisure as a Methodist preacher. Many good stories are told of him. It was he who said to the Duke of Kent, when the latter informed him of the issue of the great battle at Vittoria, "If Lord Wellington had had any other bootmaker than myself he would never have had his great and constant successes, for my boots and my prayers bring him out of all his difficulties." When Horace Churchill entered his shop and complained in no moderate words of a pair of boots, vowing he would never employ him again, Hoby quickly turned the tables. "John, close the shutters," he cried to an assistant, affecting a woebegone look. "It is all over with us. I must shut up shop. Ensign Churchill withdraws his custom from me." Sir John Shelley once showed him a pair of top-boots that had split in several places. "How did that happen, Sir John?" "Why, in walking to my stable," the customer explained. "Walking to your stable!" Hoby exclaimed, not troubling to suppress a sneer. "I made the boots for riding, not walking."9

It is but a step from boots to blacking, an article to which the dandies devoted much attention. Lieutenant-Colonel Kelly, of the First Foot Guards, was famous for his well-varnished boots. After his death, which occurred in a fire owing to his efforts to save his favourite boots, all the men about town were anxious to secure the services of his valet, who alone knew the secret of the blacking. Brummell found the man and asked his wages. The Colonel had given him a hundred and fifty pounds a year, but now he required two hundred. "Well, if you will make it guineas," said the Beau, "*I* shall be happy to attend upon *you*!" Lord Petersham spent a great deal of time in making a particular kind of blacking which he believed would eventually supersede all others, and Brummell declared, "My blacking ruins me; it is made with the finest champagne." But Brummell must not be taken too seriously. He was a master *poseur*, and many of his critics have fallen into the error of taking him literally. Thus it has apparently never occurred to his biographers to think he was joking when, in reply to a lady who inquired what allowance she should make her son who was about to enter the world, he assured her that, *with economy*, her son could dress on eight hundred a year. They merely comment upon his terribly extravagant ideas. Again, when the Beau, speaking of a boy, said with apparent earnestness, "Really, I did my best for the young man; I once gave him my arm all the way from White's to Watier's"—about a hundred yards—they discuss his enormous conceit!

There are several accounts of the cause of the rupture of the intimacy between Brummell and the Prince. It is certain, however, that the story of "Wales, ring the bell," has no foundation. "I was on such intimate terms with the Prince that if we had been alone I could have asked him without offence to ring the bell," Brummell said; "but with a third person in the room I should never have done so. I knew the Regent too well." The story was true in so far as the order, "Wales, ring the bell," was given at the royal supper-table by a lad who had taken too much to drink. The Prince did ring the bell, and when the servants came, told them, good-humouredly enough, to "put that drunken boy to bed." One authority says the quarrel arose because Brummell spoke sarcastically of Mrs Fitzherbert, another because he spoke in her favour when the Prince was bestowing his smiles in another quarter. The Beau believed it was because of remarks concerning both Mrs Fitzherbert and the Prince. There is no doubt Brummell did allow himself considerable licence of speech, and having a ready wit, was not inclined to forego its use.

A curious tale was told by General Sir Arthur Upton to Gronow. It seems that the first estrangement did not last long. Brummell played whist at White's Club one night, and won from George Harley Drummond10 the sum of twenty thousand pounds. The Duke of York told the Prince of the incident, and the Beau was again invited to Carlton House. "At the commencement of the dinner matters went off smoothly; but Brummell, in his joy at finding himself with his old friend, became excited, and drank too much wine. His Royal Highness—who wanted to avenge himself for an insult he had received at Lady Cholmondeley's ball, when the Beau, looking towards the Prince, said to Lady Worcester, 'Who is your fat friend?'—had invited him to dinner merely out of a desire for revenge. The Prince, therefore, pretended to be affronted with Brummell's hilarity, and said to his brother, the Duke of York, who was present, 'I think we had better order Mr Brummell's carriage before he gets drunk'; whereupon he rang the bell, and Brummell left the royal presence." As Sir Arthur was present at the dinner, there can be no doubt as to the facts; and, knowing the character of the royal host as we do, there is no reason to doubt that he invited a guest to insult him. That is quite of a piece with his conduct on other occasions; but it seems certain that the motive that spurred the Prince on to revenge was not that attributed to him. Of all the versions of the "Who's your fat friend?" episode, that given by the General is the least likely. Inaccurate, too, is Raikes when he tells of Brummell asking the famous question of Jack Lee in St James's Street, after the latter had been seen speaking to the Prince.

The true story is the following: A dandies' ball was to be given by Lord Alvanley, Sir Henry Mildmay, Henry Pierrepoint and Brummell to celebrate a great run of luck at hazard. The question of inviting the Prince was mooted, but it was negatived because all felt sure it would be declined, since he was not on friendly terms with Brummell. The Prince, however, sent an intimation that he desired to be present, and of course a formal invitation was despatched. The four hosts assembled at the door to do honour to their royal guest, who shook hands with three of them, but looked Brummell full in the face and passed on without any sign of recognition. Then it was, before the Prince was out of hearing, that Brummell turned to his neighbour and asked with apparent nonchalance, "Alvanley, who's your fat friend?"

After this there was war to the death, and Brummell, who was a good fighter, did not miss any opportunity to wound his powerful antagonist. He was passing down Pall Mall when the Regent's carriage drew up at a picture gallery. The sentries saluted, and, keeping his back to the carriage, Brummell took the salute as if to himself. The Prince could not hide his anger from the bystanders, for he looked upon any slight to his dignity as rather worse than high treason. The foes met again later on in the waiting-room at the opera. An eye-witness has described the *rencontre*. "The Prince of Wales, who always came out rather before the performance concluded, was waiting for his carriage. Presently Brummell came out, talking eagerly to some friends, and, not seeing the Prince or his party, he took up a position near the checktaker's bar. As the crowd flowed out, Brummell was gradually pressed backwards, until he was all but driven against the Regent, who distinctly saw him, but of course would not move. In order to stop him, therefore, and prevent actual collision, one of the Prince's suite tapped him on the back, when Brummell immediately turned sharply round, and saw there was not much more than a foot between his nose and the Prince of Wales's. I watched him with intense curiosity, and observed that his countenance did not change in the slightest degree, nor did his head move; they looked straight into each other's eyes, the Prince evidently amazed and annoyed. Brummell, however, did not quail, or show the least embarrassment. He receded quite quietly, and backed slowly step by step till the crowd closed between them, never once taking his eyes off those of the Prince." Moore, in the *Twopenny Post Bag*, commemorated the quarrel in his parody of the letter from the Prince of Wales to the Duke of York, in which he says:

"I indulge in no hatred, and wish there may come ill

To no mortal, except, now I think on't, Beau Brummell,

Who declared t'other day, in a superfine passion,

He'd cut me and bring the old King into fashion."

Brummell contrived to hold his own until he took to card-playing. His patrimony of thirty thousand pounds was insufficient to justify him in entering the lists with his companions. It was the case of the earthenware pot and the iron pots. At first he was unsuccessful, and as he was not then addicted to games of chance, his depression was very great. Walking home from a club with Tom Raikes, he was lamenting his bad fortune, when he saw something bright in the roadway. He stooped and picked up a crooked sixpence. "This," he said to his companion with great cheerfulness, "is the harbinger of good luck." He drilled a hole in it and fastened it to his watch-chain. The talisman worked, and he won thirty thousand pounds in the next two years.

Fortune deserted him; but he did not lose even a third of his winnings, and Raikes, in his "Memoirs," remarks that he was never more surprised than when in 1816, one morning, Brummell confided to him that his situation had become so desperate that he must fly the country that night, and by stealth. He had lived above his income, had got into debt, and then had fallen into the hands of the notorious usurers, Howard and Gibbs. Other money-lenders may have had claims upon him; for when it was said to Alvanley that if Brummell had remained in London something might have been done for him by his friends, the witty peer made a *bon mot*: "He has done quite right to be off; it was Solomon's judgment."11

He went no farther than Calais. "Here I am *restant* for the present, and God knows solitary enough is my existence; of that, however, I should not complain, for I can always employ resources within myself, was there not a worm that will not sleep, called *conscience*, which all my endeavours to distract, all the strength of coffee, with which I constantly fumigate my unhappy brains, and all the native gaiety of the fellow who brings it to me, cannot lull to indifference beyond the moment; but I will not trouble you upon that subject." He wrote to Tom Raikes on 22nd May 1816, soon after his arrival: "You would be surprised to find the sudden change and transfiguration which one week has accomplished in my life and *propriâ personâ*. I am punctually off the pillow at half-past seven in the morning. My first object—melancholy, indeed, it may be in its nature—is to walk to the pier-head, and take my distant look at England. This you may call weakness; but I am not yet sufficiently master of those feelings which may be called indigenous to resist the impulse. The rest of my day is filled up with strolling an hour or two round the ramparts of this dismal town, in reading, and the study of that language which must hereafter be my own, for never more shall I set foot in my own country. I dine at five, and my evening has as yet been occupied in writing letters. The English I have seen here—and many of them known to me—I have cautiously avoided; and with the exception of Sir W. Bellingham and Lord Blessington, who have departed, I have not exchanged a word. Prince Esterhazy was here yesterday, and came into my room unexpectedly without my knowing he was here. He had the good nature to convey several letters for me upon his return to London. So much for my life hitherto on this side of the water."

At first he put up at the famous Dessein's, but soon he went into apartments at the house of M. Leleux. His friends came to the rescue—Alvanley, Worcester, Sefton, no doubt Raikes too, and others—and sent him a good round sum of money. But his habits had grown upon him, and he could not live economically. If he saw buhl or marqueterie or Sèvres china that he liked he bought it; and he could not accustom himself to the penny-wise economies of life. He would not give way to despair, and, naturally high-spirited, he fought bravely against depression. He wished to be appointed consul at Calais, and his friends' influence would have secured him the position, but no vacancy occurred.

He had a gleam of hope on hearing of the accession to the throne of his old companion. "He is at length King," he wrote; "will his past resentments still attach themselves to his Crown? An indulgent amnesty of former peccadilloes should be the primary grace influencing newly throned sovereignty; at least towards those who were once distinguished by his more intimate protection. From my experience, however, of the personage in question, I must doubt any favourable relaxation of those stubborn prejudices which have, during so many years, operated to the total exclusion of one of his *élèves* from the royal notice: that unfortunate—I need not particularise. You ask me how I am going on at Calais. Miserably! I am exposed every hour to all the turmoil and jeopardy that attended my latter days in England. I bear up as well as I can; and when the mercy and patience of my claimants are exhausted I shall submit without resistance to bread and water and straw. I cannot decamp a second time."12

The new King made no sign. But soon came the news that he was going abroad, and would stay a night at Calais. The pulse of the exiled dandy must have beat quickly. It was the time for forgiveness; and, after all, his offence had not been very rank. If there were generosity in the heart of the monarch, surely, surely he would hold out the right hand of fellowship to the vanquished foe. The meeting came about unexpectedly. Brummell went for a walk out of the town in the opposite direction to that on which the King would enter it. On his return he tried to get across the street, but the crowd was so great that he remained perforce on the opposite side. The King's carriage passed close to him. "Good God, Brummell!" George cried in a loud voice. Then Brummell, who was hat in hand at the time, crossed the road, pale as death, and entered his room.

George dined in the evening at Dessein's, and Brummell sent his valet to make the punch, giving him to take over a bottle of rare old maraschino, the King's favourite liqueur. The next morning all the suite called except Bloomfield, and each man tried to persuade him to ask for an audience. Brummell signed his name in the visitors' book. His pride would let him do no more. He had taken the first steps; would the King send for him?

George left without a word. Afterwards he actually boasted he had been to Calais without seeing Brummell! So the men went their ways, never to meet again. The King had won. He had seen his old friend, his old foe—which you will—his old comrade, beaten, bankrupt, humbled, and he had passed him by. The King had won, yet perhaps for once it was better to be the vanquished than to win at such a price. Perhaps in the last years of his life George thought once more of Brummell, as himself half blind, half mad, utterly friendless, he went down to the grave unwept and unhonoured.

Others were more generous than the King. The Duke of Wellington invited two successive Ministers for Foreign Affairs to do something for the exile. Both hesitated on the ground that his Majesty might disapprove, whereupon Wellington went to Windsor and spoke to the King, "who had made objections, abusing Brummell—said he was a damned fellow and had behaved very ill to him (the old story—*moi, moi, moi*); but after having let him run his tether, he had at last extracted his consent." Still, nothing was done until after Charles Greville was at Calais in 1830: "There I had a long conversation with Brummell about his consulship, and was moved by his account of his own distresses to write to the Duke of Wellington and ask him to do what he could for him. I found him in his old lodging, dressing—some pretty pieces of old furniture in the room, an entire toilet of silver, and a large green macaw perched on the back of a tattered silk chair with faded gilding—full of gaiety, impudence, and misery."

The consulate at Caen, to which a salary of four hundred a year was attached, was secured for him. Brummell arranged that part of his income should be set aside to pay his debts (which amounted to about a thousand pounds), and his creditors allowed him to leave Calais. He had not long been installed when he wrote a formal letter to Lord Palmerston, then Foreign Secretary, stating that the place was a sinecure and the duties so trifling that he should recommend its abolition. It has never been made clear why he took this remarkable step. Was it in the hope of being appointed to a better position? Was it in the desire to evade the payment of his debts? Was it honesty? Whatever the cause, his action recoiled on himself. Lord Palmerston was regretfully compelled to take the consul at his word, and the place was reduced.

Brummell continued to live at Caen; but, being without resources, he sank deeper into debt, and in 1835 his creditors put him into prison. For the last time his friends came to his assistance. William IV. subscribed a hundred pounds. Palmerston gave twice that amount from the public purse. Enough was obtained to secure his liberation and to settle upon him an annuity of one hundred and twenty pounds. Soon he sank into a state of imbecility, and he ended his days in the asylum Bon Sauveur. He died on 30th March 1840.

A moral can easily be drawn from the story of this unfortunate man, and many writers have dwelt upon the lesson it furnishes. Yet there were many worse than he in the circle of which he was the arbiter. He lived his life: he paid the price. Let him rest in peace.

With the departure from England of Brummell the cult of the dandy began to decline. Count D'Orsay the Magnificent, however, galvanised it into fashion for a while. "He is a grand creature," Gronow described him; "beautiful as the Apollo Belvedere in his outward form; full of health, life, spirits, wit, and gaiety; radiant and joyous; the admired of all admirers."

He had an amusing *naïveté* in speaking of his personal advantages. "You know, my dear friend, I am not on a par with my antagonist," he said to his second on the eve of a duel. "He is a very ugly man, and if I wound him in the face he won't look much the worse for it; but on my side it ought to be agreed that he shall not aim higher than my chest, for if my face should be spoiled *ce serait vraiment dommage.*"

The dandies of a later day were but poor things—pinchbeck. Captain Gronow, in his youth a *beau* of no mean order, pours contempt upon their pretensions in no measured terms. "How unspeakably odious—with a few brilliant exceptions, such as Alvanley and others—were the dandies of forty years ago [1822]! They were generally middle-aged, some even elderly, men, had large appetites and weak digestions, gambled freely, and had no luck. They hated everybody and abused everybody, and would sit together in White's bay window or the pit-boxes at the opera weaving tremendous crammers. They swore a good deal, never laughed, had their own particular slang, looked hazy after dinner, and had most of them been patronised at one time or other by Brummell and the Prince Regent. . . . They gloried in their shame, and believed in nothing good or noble or elevated. Thank Heaven, that miserable race of used-up dandies has long been extinct! May England never look upon their like again!"

The prayer may well be echoed. The bad influence of the dandies can scarcely be over-estimated; and the effect upon their own class of society was terrible. Their morals were contemptible, and they were without principle. Prodigality was their creed, gambling their religion. The list of those who died beggared is not much longer than the list of those who died by their own hands. They indulged in no manly exercises, and devoted their days to their personal decoration and to the card-table. Extravagance of all kinds was fashionable. Clothes, canes, snuff-boxes, must be expensive to be worthy of such distinguished folk, whose sole aim it was to outvie each other. A guinea was the least that could be given to the butler when dining out; but this was an improvement upon the day when Pope, finding it cost him five guineas in tips whenever he dined with the Duke of Montagu, informed that nobleman he could not dine with him in future unless he sent him an order for the tribute-money.

There was Wellesley Pole, who, after the opera, gave magnificent dinners at his home at Wanstead, where rare dishes were served and the greatest luxury obtained. He married Miss Tylney Pole, who brought him fifty thousand a year; and he died a beggar. There was "Golden Ball" Hughes, with forty thousand a year, who, when the excitements of the gaming-room were not to be had, would play battledore and shuttlecock through the whole night, backing himself for immense sums. He married a beautiful Spanish *danseuse*, Mercandotti, who appeared in London in 1822. Whereupon Ainsworth made an epigram:

"The fair damsel is gone, and no wonder at all

That, bred to the dance, she is gone to a Ball."

The honeymoon was spent at Oatlands, purchased from the Duke of York. It was thought to be a foolish investment; but when Hughes fell upon evil days he was able to sell the estate for a large sum, as the new railway skirted it, and speculative builders were anxious to acquire the land, and so some of his old prosperity returned. There was Lord Fife, an intimate friend of the Regent's, who spent forty thousand pounds on Mademoiselle Noblet the dancer. A chapter would not suffice for an account of the vicious and foolish habits of these men.

The clubs were then a far more important feature in social life than they are to-day. They were accessible only to those who were in society, which in those days was exclusive, and consisted of a comparatively small body in which everyone knew everyone else, if not personally, at least by name. There were then no clubs for professional men save those of the first rank, or for merchants, or for the *hoi polloi*.

In more or less direct rivalry with the clubs were some of the hotels, and men such as Wellington, Nelson, Collingwood and Sir John Moore used them as a meeting-place—at the beginning of the eighteenth century about fifteen in number, not including, of course, the large coaching inns, coffee, eating, and the *à la mode* beef houses, most of which had beds for customers. First and foremost of these, kept by a French *chef*, Jacquiers, who had served Louis XVIII. and Lord Darnley, was the Clarendon, built upon a portion of the gardens of Clarendon House, between Bond Street and Albemarle Street, in each of which the hotel had a frontage. This was the only place in England where a French dinner was served that was worthy of mention in the same breath with those obtainable in Paris at the Maison Doré or Rocher de Cancalle's. The prices were very high. Dinner cost three or four pounds a head, and a bottle of claret or champagne was not obtainable under a guinea. A suite of apartments was reserved for banquets, and it was in these that the famous dinner, ordered by Count D'Orsay, was given to Lord Chesterfield when he resigned the office of Master of the Buckhounds. Covers were laid for thirty, and the bill, exclusive of wine, came to one hundred and eighty guineas.

Limmer's was another well-known hotel, the resort of the sporting world and of rich country squires. It was gloomy and ill-kept, but renowned for its plain English cooking and world-famous for gin-punch. The clergy went to Ibbetson's, naval men to Fladong's in Oxford Street, and army officers and men about town to Stephen's in Bond Street. Most of these hostelries had their regular frequenters, and strangers were not, as a rule, encouraged to use them as a house of call.

Clubs were few in number. There was "The Club" of Johnson; the Cocoa-Tree, which arose out of the Tory Chocolate House of Anne's reign; the Royal Naval Club, a favourite haunt of the Duke of Clarence; and the Eccentrics, which numbered among its members such well-known men as Fox, Sheridan, Lord Petersham, Brougham, Lord Melbourne, and Theodore Hook. Graham's was second rate; nor was Arthur's in the first flight. When Arthur died, his son-in-law, Mackreth, became the proprietor. He prospered, became a member of Parliament in 1774, and was afterwards knighted. His name is preserved in a very good epigram:

"When Mackreth served in Arthur's crew,

He said to Rumbold, 'Black my shoe';

To which he answered, 'Ay, Bob.'

But when return'd from India's land,

And grown too proud to brook command,

He sternly answered, 'Nay, Bob."'13

An institution of a somewhat different class was the Beefsteak Society, which flourished so long ago as the early years of the eighteenth century. The Prince of Wales became a member in 1785, when the number of the Steaks was increased from twenty-four to twenty-five in order to admit him; and subsequently the Dukes of Clarence and Sussex were elected. The bill of fare was restricted to beefsteaks, and the beverages to port wine and punch; but the cuisine on at least one occasion left something to be desired, for when, in 1830, the English Opera House was burnt down, Greville remarked in his diary: "I trust the paraphernalia of the Beefsteak Club perished with the rest, for the enmity I bear that society for the dinner they gave me last year." Charles Morris was the bard of the Beefsteak Society, and he has come down to posterity on the strength of four lines:

"In town let me live then, in town let me die,

For in truth I can't relish the country, not I.

If one must have a villa in summer to dwell,

Oh, give me the sweet, shady side of Pall Mall!"

In spite of his prayer, he spent the last years of his life in the rural retreat of Brockham, in Surrey, in a little place presented to him by his fellow-Steak, the Duke of Norfolk. He lived to the great age of ninety-two, and was so hale and hearty and cheerful that, not long before his death, Curran said to him, "Die when you will, Charles, you will die in your youth."

Lumley S^t. George Skeffington Esqr.

The greatest club of its day was Almack's, at 5 Pall Mall, founded in 1740 by Macall, a Scotsman. This institution was nicknamed the "Macaroni Club," owing to the fashion of its members; and Gibbon remarked that "the style of living, though somewhat expensive, is exceedingly pleasant, and notwithstanding the rage of play, I have found more entertainment and rational society here than in any other club to which I belong." The high play, which was the bane of half the English aristocracy, ruined many members. The club fell upon evil days, and was absorbed by Brooks's.

White's and Brooks's took the place of Almack's. The former, established in 1698 as "White's Chocolate-House," five doors from the bottom of the west side of St James's Street, became a club in 1755, when it moved to No. 38, on the opposite side of the street. It was owned successively by Arthur Mackreth, John Martindale, and in 1812 by Raggett, whose son eventually inherited it. Brooks's was founded by a wine merchant and money-lender of the name, who has been described by Tickell in verses addressed to

Sheridan, when Charles James Fox was to give a supper at his rooms near the club:

"Derby shall send, if not his plate, his cooks;

And know, I've bought the best champagne from Brooks,

From liberal Brooks, whose speculative skill

Is hasty credit and a distant bill;

Who, nursed in clubs, disdains a vulgar trade,

Exults to trust, and blushes to be paid."

Both clubs, although more or less instituted for the purpose of gambling, were at first political. White's, however, soon took down the Tory flag and received members without reference to their political opinions. Brooks's, on the other hand, remained true to its Whig traditions; and it was to counterbalance the influence of this institution—the "Reform" of that time—that the Carlton Club was organised by Lord Clanwilliam and others. These, with Boodles', were the great resorts of the dandies; and the bay window at White's, when Brummell was the lion, was one of the sights of the town. The Prince of Wales was a member of Brooks's; but when his boon companions Tarleton and Jack Payne were blackballed he withdrew, and on his own account founded a new club, of which the manager was Weltzie, his house-steward.

Watier's, the great macao gambling-house, was founded in 1807; but play was very high, and it lasted only for twelve years. According to Gronow it came into existence in a somewhat curious way. When some members of White's and Brooks's were dining at Carlton House, the Prince of Wales asked what sort of dinners were served at these institutions. One of the guests complained: "The eternal joints and beefsteaks, the boiled fowl with oyster sauce, and an apple-tart. This is what we have, sir, at our clubs, and very monotonous fare it is." The Prince sent for Watier, his *chef*, and asked if he would take a house and organise a club-dinner. Watier was willing. The scheme was carried out, and the club was famed for its exquisite cuisine.

Another and more circumstantial account of the founding of the club is given by Raikes. He says it was originally instituted as a harmonic meeting by the Maddochs, Calverts and Lord Headfort, who took a house in Piccadilly, at the corner of Bolton Street, and engaged Watier as master of the revels. "This destination of the club was soon changed. The dinners were so *recherché* and so much talked of in town that all the young men of fashion and fortune became members of it. The catches and glees were then superseded by cards and dice; the most luxurious dinners were furnished at any price, as the deep play at night rendered all charges a matter of indifference. Macao was the constant game, and thousands passed from one to another with as much facility as marbles."

The Duke of York was a member of Watier's, and so too was Byron, who christened it "The Dandy Club."

Another member was Robert Bligh, whose eccentricities were already verging upon insanity. One night, at the macao-table, Brummell was losing heavily, and in an affected tone of tragedy he called to a waiter to bring him a pistol. Thereupon Bligh, who was his *vis-à-vis*, produced from his coat pockets a pair of loaded pistols, and laying them on the table, said, "Mr Brummell, if you are really desirous to put a period to your existence, I am extremely happy to offer you the means without troubling the waiter." The feelings of the members may be imagined when the knowledge was forced upon them that in their midst was a madman who carried loaded firearms.

Brummell, Raikes has recorded, was the supreme dictator at Watier's, "the club's perpetual president." At the height of his prosperity, one night when he entered, the macao-table was full. Sheridan was there trying his luck with a few pounds he could ill spare, for he had fallen upon evil days. Brummell, whose good luck was notorious at this time, offered to take Sheridan's seat and go shares in his deal. He added two hundred pounds in counters to the ten pounds in front of him, took the cards, dealt, and in a quarter of an hour had won fifteen hundred pounds. Then he left the table and divided his gains with Sheridan. "Go home, Sheridan," he said quietly; "go home and give your wife and brats a supper, and never play again." It is good to be able to record a generous act, delicately done, of a much-abused man.

Of Brummell's witty insolence mention has already been made, but the laugh was once at least against him. He was at the card-table playing with Combe the brewer, an Alderman who had passed the chair. "Come, Mashtub," he said, being the caster, "what do you set?" "Twenty-five guineas." "Well, then, have at the mare's pony" (twenty-five guineas). The game progressed, and Brummell won twelve times in succession. "Thank you, Alderman," he said; "for the future I shall never drink any porter but yours." "I wish, sir," retorted Combe, "that every other blackguard in London would say the same."

Everybody played cards in those days. Even at the quiet Court of "Farmer" George the tables were set out in the Queen's drawing-rooms. Ladies gambled with as much zest as their husbands and brothers, and at the end of the eighteenth century several held gaming-tables. "Faro goes on as briskly as ever; those who have not fortune enough of their own to live on have recourse to this profitable game in order to raise contributions on their friends," wrote Anthony Storer to Lord Auckland in 1791. "The ladies are all embarked in banks. Mrs Strutt, Lady Archer, Mrs Hobart, Lady Elizabeth Luttrell (sister of the Duchess of Cumberland), are avowed bankers; others, I suppose, are secretly concerned." Information was laid against Lady Archer and Lady Buckinghamshire, who were convicted and fined; and Lord Kenyon, delivering judgment in another case, actually declared that if any titled ladies were found guilty of the offence before him they should stand in the pillory. No one was bold enough to test the sincerity of the threat. As *The Morning Post* put it in its issue for 15th January 1800: "Society has reason to rejoice in the complete downfall of the Faro Dames who were so long the disgrace of human nature. Their *die* is cast, and their *odd tricks* avail no longer. The *game* is up, and very few of them have *cut* with *honours*."

Play was taken very seriously, for the stakes were always heavy, and conversation was resented. Sir Philip Francis came to Brooks's wearing for the first time the ribbon of the Order of the Bath, for which Fox had recommended him. "So this is the way they have rewarded you at last," remarked Roger Wilbraham, coming up to the whist-table. "They have given you a little bit of red ribbon for your services, Sir Philip, have they? A pretty bit of red ribbon to hang about your neck; and that satisfies you, does it? Now, I wonder what I shall have. What do you think they will give me, Sir Philip?" "A halter, I trust and hope!" roared the infuriated player.

It was at Almack's, and later at White's, Brooks's, Weltzie's and Watier's, that the heaviest play prevailed. It is no exaggeration to say that during the long sittings at macao, hazard and faro many tens of thousands changed hands. Nelson won three hundred pounds at a gaming-table when he was seventeen; but he was so horrified when he reflected if he had lost he could not have paid that he never played again. Pitt gambled, and George Selwyn, and Fox, who was always unlucky.

"At Almack's, of pigeons I'm told there are flocks,

But it's thought the completest is one Mr Fox.

If he touches a card, if he rattles a box,

Away fly the guineas of this Mr Fox."

Fox lost two hundred thousand pounds in a night. Once he played for twenty-two hours and lost five hundred pounds an hour. It was he who said that the greatest pleasure in life, after winning, was losing. His bad luck was notorious, and Walpole wondered what he would do when he had sold the estates of all his friends. How Fox contrived to make a great reputation as a statesman, considering his mode of life, is truly remarkable. It was noticed that he did not shine in the debate on the Thirty-Nine Articles (6th February 1772). Walpole thought it could not be wondered at. "He had sat up playing at hazard at Almack's from Tuesday evening, the 4th, till five in the afternoon of Wednesday, 5th. An hour before, he had recovered twelve thousand pounds that he had lost, and by dinner, which was at five o'clock, he had ended losing eleven thousand pounds. On the Thursday he spoke in the above debate, went to dinner at half-past eleven at night, from there to White's, where he drank till seven the next morning; thence to Almack's, where he won six thousand pounds, and between three and four in the afternoon he set out for Newmarket. His brother Stephen lost ten thousand pounds two nights after, and Charles eleven thousand pounds more on the 13th, so that in three nights the two brothers, the eldest not twenty-five, lost thirty-two thousand pounds." One night when Fox had been terribly unlucky, Topham Beauclerk followed him to his rooms to offer consolation, expecting to find him perhaps stretched on the floor bewailing his losses, perhaps plunged into moody despair. He was surprised to find him reading Herodotus. "What would you have me do?" he asked his astonished visitor. "I have lost my last shilling."

"But, hark! the voice of battle shouts from far,

The Jews and Macaronis are at war

The Jews prevail, and thund'ring from the stocks,

They seize, they bind, they circumcise Charles Fox."

They were good losers in those days, and it was a very necessary quality for the majority to possess, since all played and most lost. Lord Carlisle (who complained of *cette lassitude de tout et de moi-même, qu'on appelle ennui*), General Fitzpatrick, "Old Q.," Lord Hertford, Lord Sefton, the Duke of York, and many others squandered vast sums in this amusement. There were not a great many winners. The Duke of Portland was one; and his and Canning's father-in-law, General Scott, won two hundred thousand pounds. It was said the success of the latter was due not only to his knowledge of the game of whist, but also to his notorious sobriety. General Fitzpatrick and Lord Robert Spencer lost all their money at Brooks's; but, the members not objecting, with borrowed capital they kept a faro bank. The bank won, and with his share of one hundred thousand pounds Lord Robert bought the estate of Woolbidding, in Sussex. He had learnt his lesson, and he never played again. There were few who had the sense to make or the strength to keep such a resolution. Mrs Delany, however, tells of a Mr Thynne "who has won this year so considerably that he has paid off all his debts, bought a house and furnished it, disposed of all his horses, hounds, etc., and struck his name out of all the expensive subscriptions." A fortunate man, too, was

Colonel Aubrey, who had the reputation of being the best whist and piquet player of his day. He made two fortunes in India and lost them both, and made a third at play from a five-pound note which he borrowed.

Another celebrated faro bank at Brooks's was that kept by Lord Cholmondeley, Mr Thompson of Grosvenor Square, Tom Stepney, and a fourth. It ruined half the town; and a Mr Paul, who had come home with a fortune from India, punting against the bank, lost ninety thousand pounds in one night, and at once went Eastward Ho! to make another. Lord Cholmondeley and Mr Thompson realised between three and four hundred thousand pounds apiece; but Stepney so frequently played against his partners that what he won on one side he lost on the other, with the result that his gains were inconsiderable.

Foreigners were made honorary members of the clubs. The Duke of Orleans ("Vile Égalité," Lady Sarah Bunbury wrote him down) carried off vast sums. During the visit of the Allied Sovereigns, Blücher, an inveterate gambler, lost twenty thousand pounds. Count Montrond, on the other hand, was a winner. "Who the deuce is this Montrond?" the Duke of York asked Upton. "They say, sir, that he is the most agreeable scoundrel and the greatest reprobate in France." "Is he, by Jove?" cried the Duke. "Then let us ask him to dinner immediately." Montrond was a witty fellow, and one of his *bon mots* has been handed down. The Bailli de Ferretti was always dressed in knee-breeches, with a cocked hat and a Court sword, the slender proportions of which resembled those of his legs. "Do tell me, my dear Bailli," said Montrond one day, "have you got three legs or three swords?"

Englishmen were not backward in playing abroad, and they assembled in great numbers at the Salon des Étrangers in Paris during the stay of the army of occupation after Waterloo. Gronow gives a long list of habitués: Henry Baring, Tom Sowerby, Henry Broadwood, Bob Arnold, Steer, Colonel Sowerby, were the most reckless plungers. Lord Thanet, who had an income of fifty thousand pounds, lost every penny he had at the *salon*. He would not stop playing when the public tables closed, and used to invite those present to remain and play hazard or écarté. One night he lost a hundred and twenty thousand pounds. His friends told him he had most probably been cheated. "Then," he said with great coolness, "I consider myself lucky not to have lost twice as much."

Prominent among gamblers, and as such deserving of special mention, was William Douglas, Earl of March and Ruglen, afterwards fourth and last Duke of Queensberry.14 Even making liberal allowance for the spirit of the age and for the state of morality in the days when he was young, he was one of the worst men of his generation; and his rank and wealth made his vices only more notorious. He was the "Degenerate Douglas" of Wordsworth's muse, and Burns damned him in verse for all time:

"How shall I sing Drumlanrig's Grace,

Discarded remnant of a race

Once great in martial story?

His forebears' virtues all contrasted,

The very name of Douglas blasted—

His that inverted glory.

Hate, envy, oft the Douglas bore;

But he has superadded more,

And sunk them in contempt.

Follies and crimes have stained the name;

But, Queensberry, thine the virgin claim—

From aught that's good exempt."

He was appointed to the Household of George III.; but when the King's malady declared itself in 1788, he, in common with many other courtiers, veered round to the side of the Prince of Wales. George recovered, and the Duke was dismissed. His profligacy was a byword, and he pursued pleasure to the end of his days. He built a palace at Richmond, where many orgies took place. But he tired of that residence, as he wearied of most people and most things. "What is there to make so much of in the Thames? I am quite tired of it. There it goes, flow, flow, flow, always the same." At the end of his days he sat on the balcony of a ground-floor room of his Piccadilly mansion, and ogled the passers-by, while a footman held a parasol over his head, and another was ready to follow and find out the residence of any pretty girl that passed. Yet "Old Q." had wit in plenty, loved music, and was not without appreciation of letters and art. One of his greatest friends was George Selwyn; and, while both accredited themselves with the paternity, neither knew which was the father of Maria Fagniani. This young lady became Selwyn's ward and the inheritrix of the greater part of his fortune, while the Duke left her his residence in Piccadilly, a villa at Richmond, and a hundred and fifty thousand pounds; and her husband, Lord Yarmouth, afterwards third Marquis of Hertford, as the Duke's residuary legatee, came into about two hundred thousand pounds.

"Old Q." was a dangerous man at the card-table. The turf had no mysteries for him. He was ever ready to bet, and he preferred to bet on something that was very nearly a certainty. He was full of resource, and his success was due at least as much to his cleverness as to his luck. His was the day of wagers, and at White's a betting-book was laid upon a table for all bets made in the building to be inserted. His name frequently occurs therein:

"*June 1751*.—Lord March wagers Captain Richard Vernon fifty guineas to twenty that Mr St Leger is married before him." The bet requires the explanatory note that "him" stands for Captain Vernon.

"*March 1784*.—The Duke of Queensberry bets Mr Grenville ten guineas to five that Mr Fox does not stand a poll for Westminster if the Parliament should be dissolved within a month from the date hereof. *N.B.*—If a coalition takes place between Mr Pitt and Mr Fox this bet is to be off." It is to be noticed that the Duke was not convinced of the sincerity of politicians.

The Duke bet Sir John Lade a thousand guineas as to which could produce a man to eat the most at one sitting. The Duke could not be present at the contest, but he received the result from a representative. "I have not time to state particulars, but merely to acquaint your Grace that your man beat his antagonist by a pig and an apple-pie." What must they have eaten!

White's betting-book is full of quaint wagers. "Lord Northington bets Mr C. Fox, June 4, 1774, that he (Mr. C. F.) is not called to the Bar before this day four years." On 11th March 1775 is an interesting entry: "Lord Bolingbroke gives a guinea to Mr Charles Fox, and is to receive a thousand from him whenever the debt of this country amounts to one hundred and seventy-one millions. Mr Fox is not to pay the thousand pounds till he is one of his Majesty's Cabinet." The following is dated 7th April 1792: "Mr Sheridan bets Lord Lauderdale and Lord Thanet twenty-five guineas each that Parliament will not consent to any more lotteries after the present one voted to be drawn in February next." Lotteries were then a regular source of revenue to the State, the average profit being about three hundred and fifty thousand pounds a year, besides many brokers' annual licences at fifty pounds. Private lotteries were forbidden by law, and required a special Act of Parliament to enable them to be drawn. The result was that the only two private lotteries were the Pigot Diamond in 1800 and Boydell's pictures five years later. Lotteries were first drawn at Guildhall and later at the Coopers' Hall, and the tickets were taken from the wheels by Bluecoat boys. The last public lottery took place in October 1826, and so Mr Sheridan lost his bet.

On 8th May 1809, "Mr G. Talbot bet Lord Charles Manners ten guineas that the Duke of Queensberry is not alive this day two years." Another entry records that "Mr C. H. Bouverie bets Mr Blackford that the Duke of

Queensberry outlives the Duke of Grafton." "Lord Mountford bets Sir John Bland twenty guineas that Nash outlives Cibber." But the bet was cancelled, because before either Nash or Cibber died the two wagerers committed suicide!

Apparently no subject was thought unfit for a bet. Wagers were made as to which of two married ladies would first give birth to a live child, and as to which of two men would marry first. They bet with equal heartiness on the duration of a Ministry or the life of a Minister, on a horse, or a dog, or a prize-fight, or a cock-fight. Walpole tells the story of a simple parson entering White's on the morning of a severe earthquake, and hearing bets laid whether the shock was caused by an earthquake or the blowing up of powder mills, went away in horror, protesting that they were such an impious set that he believed if the Last Trump were to sound they would bet puppet-show against Judgment!

All other English clubs where gaming took place fade into insignificance before Crockford's. Crockford was originally a fishmonger at the old Bulkshop next door to Temple Bar Without, and later a "leg" at Newmarket. He became part-proprietor of a gambling-house, and with his partner, at a twenty-four hours' sitting, he won a hundred thousand pounds from five punters, including Lord Thanet, Lord Granville and Ball Hughes. He then built the famous palace in St James's Street opposite to White's.

"No one can describe the splendour and excitement of the early days of Crockford's," Gronow relates. "A supper of the most exquisite kind, prepared by the famous Ude, and accompanied by the best wines in the world, together with every luxury of the season, was provided gratis. The members of the club included all the celebrities of England, from the Duke of Wellington to the youngest ensign of the Guards; and at the gay and festive board, which was constantly replenished from midnight till early dawn, the most brilliant sallies of wit, the most agreeable conversation, the most interesting anecdotes, interspersed with grave political discussions and acute logical reasoning on every conceivable subject, proceeded from the soldiers, scholars, statesmen, poets, and men of pleasure, who, when the House was 'up' and balls and parties at an end, delighted to finish their evenings with a little supper and a good deal of hazard at old Crockey's. The tone of the club was excellent. A most gentleman-like feeling prevailed, and none of the rudeness, familiarity, and ill-breeding which disgrace some of the minor clubs of the present day would have been tolerated for a moment."

The whole establishment was organised on a scale of wonderful magnificence; and to keep it select, the election of members was controlled by a committee. Talleyrand, Pozzo di Borgo, General Alava, Esterhazy, and other ambassadors belonged to it; the Duke of Wellington, Lord Raglan, Lord Anglesea, Sir Hussey Vivian, Disraeli, Bulwer, Croker, Horace Twiss, and, as a matter of course, Lord Alvanley and Count D'Orsay. Though many members never touched a card, Crockford with his hazard bank won a sum estimated at between one million two hundred thousand and two million pounds, or, as a contemporary put it very neatly, "the whole of the ready money of the then existing generation." He died worth seven hundred thousand pounds, after having sustained heavy losses in mining and other speculations. The retirement of Crockford marks an epoch, for after that date the craze for gambling on a vast scale slowly but surely died out. By this time, however, it had done as much harm to the aristocracy as the South Sea Bubble did to the general public.

A Forgotten Satirist: "Peter Pindar"

The amusing banter of Mr E. V. Lucas and Mr C. L. Graves, and the delightful parody of Mr Owen Seaman, are the nearest approach that England can now show to the satirical productions for which it was once famous. Indeed, we are becoming an amiable race, developing, or at least feigning, the milk of human kindness to such an extent that even modern caricature can scarcely be distinguished from portraiture, and only Mr Max Beerbohm flings the tomahawk of pictorial satire. A study of the lampoons and the vigorous personal onslaughts in prose and verse of the Georgian days, however, gives us pause for reflection whether we refrain from such practices because of our improved manners or increasing effeminacy: though, perhaps, it may be attributed largely to the signed review which makes it difficult, in these days of numerous literary associations, for a sociable or a nervous scholar to gibbet his erring brethren with an acerbity once general. Certain it is that current criticism is for the most part the art of saying pleasant things graciously, while our excursions into the personal element are usually headed "Appreciations." Whatever the cause, it is a sad thought for militant spirits that a wave of politeness has engulfed the heretofore blunt, outspoken John Bull, that typical figure, of which—it is pathetic to note in these days of unsuppressed emotion—we are still so proud.

The most casual incursion into Georgian history reveals a great mass of almost forgotten satirical productions, all of it trenchant, most of it coarse and not a little scurrilous, indeed, but much of it readable and amusing. There were scores of virile pamphleteers in the pay of Ministers and Oppositions, as well as a number of independent writers of lampoons on all sorts and conditions of men and things. The best of the latter class was Charles Churchill, the famous author of "The Rosciad" and of those terrible onslaughts on Hogarth and Sandwich, on Martin and other small fry. His mantle was in due course assumed by Wolcot, who, though scarcely remembered to-day, was a man of considerable talent and extensive knowledge, and, though of course without the genius of his predecessor, was widely read, enjoyed a vast popularity, and undoubtedly influenced a great body of people.

John Wolcot, the son of a country surgeon, was born in May 1738. He was educated at various schools of no great repute, and in the early twenties paid a lengthy visit to France, for the inhabitants of which land he conceived the insular prejudice usual in his day:

"I never will put Merit on the rack:

No; yet, I own, I hate the shrugging dogs.

I've lived among them, eat their frogs,

And vomited them up, thank God, again."

He studied medicine in London until 1764, when he went as assistant to his uncle, John Wolcot of Fowey, taking a Scotch Degree of Doctor of Medicine three years later, immediately after which, his distant connection, Sir William Trelawny, going to Jamaica as Governor, he accompanied him as physician. In that island he saw little or no prospect of securing a paying practice, and paid a flying visit to England in 1769 to take holy orders. On his return to Jamaica he found that the lucrative living for which he had been destined, had, contrary to expectation, not been vacated, whereupon, after holding a minor clerical post for a few months, he reverted to his old profession, and obtained the post of physician-general to the troops. Sir William Trelawny died at Spanish Town in 1772, and Wolcot again came to England, where he established himself as a doctor at Truro, but, after disputes with his medical *confrères* and the Corporation, removed in 1779 to Helstone and then to Exeter.

Wolcot abandoned the practice of medicine in 1781, when he came to London, urged to this step partly by the desire to advance the prospects of his *protégé*, Opie, the painter, and partly by the desire to establish himself there as a man of letters. The last project was not so mad as it may have appeared to his country neighbours, for under the pseudonym of "Peter Pindar" he had already obtained some success with the publication of a "Poetical Epistle to Reviewers" in 1778, in which he declared:

"In Sonnet, Ode, and Legendary Tale,

Soon will the press my tuneful Works display."

He fulfilled this promise, and in 1782 issued "Lyric Odes to the Royal Academicians for 1782," by "Peter Pindar, Esq., a distant relative of the Poet of Thebes and Laureat to the Academy," which were at once so successful, that in quick succession came from his fertile pen, "More Lyric Odes to the Royal Academicians for 1783," "Lyric Odes for 1785," and, in 1786, "Farewell Odes to Academicians." These vigorous verses attracted much attention, for the critic was outspoken in his dislikes, and lashed with the utmost contempt "George's idol," West, and other fashionable artists; though he showed his discrimination by praising the works of Gainsborough, Reynolds ("Of whose fine art I own myself a lover"), and of the unfairly neglected Richard Wilson ("By Britain left in poverty to pine"):

"But honest Wilson, never mind;

Immortal praises thou shalt find,

And for a dinner have no cause to fear.

Thou start'st at my prophetic rhymes:

Don't be impatient for those times;

Wait till thou hast been dead a hundred year."

It was not because Wolcot had exhausted this vein (for he returned to it again and again, even in 1808 having "One more Peep at the Royal Academy") that he looked for another theme, but that he discovered, so long as he wrote on art and artists, let him be never so humorous, he would have to be content with praise alone for his reward. No man cared less for money than he, but he certainly thought the labourer worthy of his hire, and, since he depended for his livelihood on his pen, it behoved him to select a subject that would appeal to a larger public. To the exceeding joy of his own and subsequent generations, he decided to exercise his humour at the expense of the King and Queen, with an occasional playful blow at a Minister.

No satirist could ask for better subjects for his wit than George III. and Queen Charlotte. The slow-witted monarch and his parsimonious consort offered every conceivable temptation to Wolcot's nimble humour, and he was not slow to take advantage of this rare chance. Of course, he was not the first in the field, but he was head and shoulders over his rivals in talent and wit, and, if he did not silence, at least he succeeded in eclipsing them. He was especially fortunate in having accurate information concerning the internal economy of the royal palaces, and, though he took a poet's licence to embroider the facts, there was always some foundation for his lampoons. Thus, when the King found a noxious insect in his plate at dinner and gave orders that everyone in the kitchens, from *chef* to scullion, should be shaved, "Peter Pindar" wrote a "heroi-comic poem," "The Lousiad," in which he gave a version of the story. "I had this (incident)," he wrote to a friend, "from the cooks themselves, with whom I dined several times at Buckingham House and Windsor, immediately after the 'shave' took place."

" 'Some spirit whispers that to Cooks I owe

The precious Visitor that crawls below;

Yes, yes, the whispering Spirit tells me true,

And soon that vengeance all the locks pursue.

Cooks, Scourers, Scullions, too, with Tails of Pig,

Shall lose their coxcomb Curls and wear a Wig.'

Thus roared the King, not Hercules so big;

And all the Palace echoed, 'Wear a Wig!' "

So successful was the first canto of "The Lousiad," which appeared in 1785, that during the next ten years four additional cantos were written, in which members of the Household and Ministers were introduced, scarified and dismissed; but the gem of the collection is the lengthy "Petition of the Cooks," which, after references to France, the Schwellenberg and Wilkes, concludes:

" 'O King, our Wives are in the Kitchen roaring,

All ready in rebellion now to rise;

They mock our humble methods of imploring,

And bid us guard against a wig surprise:

"*Yours* is the hair," they cry, "th' Almighty gave ye,

And not a King in Christendom should shave you.' "

'Lo! on th' event the World impatient looks,

And thinks the joke is carried much too far;

Then pray, Sir, listen to your faithful Cooks,

Nor in the Palace breed a Civil War:

Loud roar our Band; and, obstinate as Pigs,

Cry, "Locks and Liberty and damn the Wigs!" ' "

Eventually the attention of the Privy Council was drawn to this poem, and that body, according to Wolcot, decided to prosecute the author, and refrained from doing so only when it discovered that the poem had its foundation in fact. "Are you sure of a verdict?" it is stated that Chancellor Thurlow inquired; "for, if not so, we shall look like a parcel of fools." Huish states emphatically that the idea of prosecuting the poet did not originate with the King; and Galt says that the effusions of the satirist produced on George "no other effect than a smile of wonder at the perverse ingenuity of the man: and the most serious thing he was ever known to say of them was on the occasion of Peter's lampooning General Carpenter, when his Majesty observed, that 'for himself he cared nothing; but he was hurt to see a worthy man calumniated, because he happened to be one of his servants.' As far as they were capable of exciting a good-natured laugh, the King enjoyed that laugh as much as any man; and when they were otherwise, as was but too often the case, he observed a dignified forbearance, leaving the author to enjoy all the triumph there might be in making a base attack on a party whom he knew to be precluded, by his dignity, from descending into the arena in his own defence."

It may, however, he doubted whether Hazlitt was accurate in stating that "the King as well as the nation delighted in the bard," for George had not a spark of humour in his composition, and was the last man in the nation to take a joke at his own expense in good part.

If, however, the King suffered in silence, the Queen was determined not to submit to similar attacks, and her solicitor warned Wolcot that if he exercised his wit against her Majesty, proceedings would at once be taken—representations that had the desired effect, although they furnished the subject for one of Peter's verses:

"Great was the Bard's desire to sing the Queen,

Vast in her soul, majestic in her mien;

But fierce George Hardinge swore, if pens or pen

Of woman, women, man or men,

In any wise or shape, in Ode or Tale,

Dared mention that *superior* Lady, lo!

The law should deal them *such* a blow!

Hang, pillory, or confine for life in jail."

When the Doctor was once reproved by an acquaintance for the liberties he took with his sovereign, "I confess there exists this difference between the King and me," he replied; "the King has been a good subject to me, but I have been a bad subject to him." This he admitted, but that he was guilty in any sense of serious offence he pooh-poohed:

"Such is the Song: and do not thou, severe,

With 'Treason! Treason!' fill a royal ear;

For gentle jokes, at times, on Queens and Kings,

Are pleasant, taking, nay, *instructive* things.

Yet *some* there are who relish not the sport,

That flutter in the sunshine of a Court;

Who, fearful Song might mar their high ambition,

Loose the gaunt Dogs of State, and bawl 'Sedition.' "

Wolcot was clever enough usually to take for his verse topics in which the public were interested, and it was to this acuteness his success with his contemporaries must be largely attributed. He attacked Lord Lonsdale when that nobleman showed a great disregard of his neighbour's rights, and "expostulated" with Hannah More, when in her "Strictures on Female Education," she wrote, "The Poets again, to do them justice, are always ready to lend a helping hand when any mischief is to be done." He inveighed against the strict enforcement of Sunday Observance, which to some extent resulted from Lady Huntingdon's petition to the King, and the Puritanism of the Methodists:

" 'No,' roars the Huntingdonian Priest; 'no, no:

Lovers are liars; love's a damned trade.

Kissing is damnable; to Hell they go:

The *Devil claws* away the rogue and jade.' "

And he gave a fanciful description of the result of the unpopular Hair-Tax, which, according to him, evoked so much disgust that, "the male sex have already sacrificed their favourite curls, to disappoint the rapacity of a minister."

Peter Pindar Esq.

"See groups of Hairdressers all idle stand,

A melancholy, mute, and mournful band;

And Barbers *eke*, who lift the crape-clod Pole,

And round and round their eyes of horror roll;

Desponding, pale, like Hosier's Ghost so white,

Who told their sorrows 'mid the morning light.

But see! each hopeless wight with fury foams;

His curling-irons breaks, and snaps his combs:

Ah! doom'd to shut their *mouths* as well as *shops*;

For dead is Custom, 'mid the world of *crops*."

Wolcot, as a defender of Mrs Fitzherbert, thought no words too strong in which to express his opinion of those who attacked her, and when John Rolle introduced the question of her marriage to the Prince of Wales in the House of Commons, he fell foul of him, and of Pitt, who supported him:

"Sick at the name of Rolle (to thee tho' dear),

The name abhorr'd by Honour's shrinking ear,

I draw reluctant from thy venal throng,

And give it mention, though it blacks my song.

How could'st thou bid that Rolle, despised by all,

On helpless beauty, like a mastiff fall;

Then meanly to correct the brute pretend,

And claim the merit of the Fair One's friend?"

He had the courage to say a good word for Paine and "The Rights of Man":

"O Paine! thy vast endeavour I admire.

How brave the hope, to set a realm on fire!

Ambition smiling praised thy giant wish.

Compared to *thee*, the man, to gain a name,

Who to Diana's temple put the flame,

A simple Minnow to the Prince of Fish."

He was fearless in his denunciation of the Duke of York, when it transpired that during the latter's occupation of the position of Commander-in-Chief, his mistress had been selling commissions and offices, and he voiced the public clamour:

"Heavens, what a dire confusion beauty makes!

The Horse Guards tremble, and old Windsor shakes.

Like bees, the mob around St Stephen's swarms;

And every street and alley feels alarms:

Men, women, coaches, gigs, each other jostle;

And thou the cause of all this horrid bustle!

Hotels and tap-rooms sound with mingled din,

And every coffee-house is on the grin.

From morn to eve, from eve to midnight dark,

Naught strikes the ear but 'Duke and Mistress Clarke.'

Nay, too, the parrot and the simple starling

Cry from their cages naught but 'Duke and Darling'!"

When, as a consequence of the inquiry, the Duke resigned, Wolcot drew a malicious picture of his loneliness:

"No longer now the Duke excites our wonder,

'Midst gun, drum, trumpet, blunderbuss and thunder;

Amidst his hosts, no more with rapture dwells

On Congreve's rockets, and on Shrapnell's shells;

But quits with scornful mien the field of Mars,

And to Sir David's genius leaves the wars.

Now in dull Windsor rides the youth is seen;

Now, in dull walks to Frogmore with the Queen;

At Oaklands, where pigs and poultry charm,

Like Cincinnatus on his Sabine farm;

Now, o'er a lonely dish in Stable Yard,

Without a friend, and (strange!) without a card!"

Wolcot sometimes contrived to combine his attacks upon art and royalty, as in "Subjects for Painters," in the introduction to which he explained that the rage for historical pictures, "so nobly rewarded by Messieurs Boydell and Macklin," tempted him to offer subjects that would be useful when the painters had exhausted Shakespeare and Milton.

"Pitt trying to unclench Britannia's fist,

Imploring money for a King;

Telling *most mournful* tales of Civil List,

The Lady's *tender* heart to wring:

Tales of expense in doctors' bills,

High price of blisters, boluses, and pills;

Long journey to Saint Paul's t'*oblige* the Nation,

And give thanks for Restoration:—

Britannia, with arch look the while,

Partaking strongly of a smile,

Pointing to that huge Dome,15 the Nation's wealth;

Where *people* sometimes place their Cash by *stealth*,

And, all so modest with their secret store,

Inform the World they're *poor*, ah! *very poor*!"

As a rule, however, Wolcot directed his lampoons against the King, whose foibles he most unmercifully laid bare. He was never weary of decrying a monarch who preferred farming to art, and whose economies were a source of scandal to the whole nation. It is said that the bitterness on this latter score arose from the King having purchased a picture from a friend of the satirist and having given him only half the market value. This, indeed, was only one instance out of many of George's meanness. He would put an artist to the expense of bringing his pictures to Windsor, and not offer to pay the carriage, even when, in the case of one such command, the cost was twenty-five pounds. He would invite eminent singers and actors to perform at Court functions and give them never a sou, thinking the honour sufficient reward.

"At length the Actress ceased to read and spout,

Where Generosity's a crying Sin:

Her curtsey dropp'd, was nodded to; came out.

So rich! How rich? As rich as she went in.

Should Mara call it cruelty, and blame

Such royal conduct, I'd cry, Fie upon her!

To Mistress Siddons freely say the same:

Sufficient for *such people* is the *honour*."

Wolcot was never weary of harping upon this unroyal quality that was common to both the sovereigns. He returned to it in the "Odes to Kien Long, Emperor of China."

"Give nothing from the Privy Purse away, I say:

Nay, should thy coffers and thy bags run o'er;

Neglect, or pension Merit on the Poor.

Give not to Hospitals; thy Name's enough:

To death-face Famine, not a pinch of snuff.

On Wealth, thy Quarry, keep a Falcon-view,

And from the very children steal their due!"

The King's love of farming for profit—a king with a Civil List of eight hundred thousand pounds and occasional special grants amounting to millions—was a subject much discussed, and not likely to escape the attention of our satirist.

". . . the note is, 'How go sheep a score?

What, what's the price of Bullocks? How sells Lamb?

I want a Boar, a Boar, I want a Boar;

I want a Bull, a Bull; I want a Ram!'

Whereas it should be this: 'I want a Bard,

To cover him with honour and reward.'"

Indeed, nothing that the King did was allowed to pass without comment. Did he go to Weymouth, "Peter Pindar" accompanied him in spirit:

"See! Cæsar's off: the dust around him hovers;

And gathering, lo, the King of Glory covers!

The Royal hubbub fills both eye and ear,

And wide-mouth'd Wonder marks the wild career."

Did George visit Samuel Whitebread's brewery, the event was duly recorded:

"Now moved the King, Queen, and Princesses, so grand,

To visit the first Brewer in the land;

Who sometimes swills his beer and grinds his meat,

In a snug corner christen'd Chiswell Street;

But oftener, charmed with *fashionable* air,

Amidst the gaudy Great of Portman Square."

Popular as such verses were, and wide as was their circulation, they were easily eclipsed in both respects by those in which the stupidity of the King was chronicled, and people, being so much amused by them, forgot that the foundation of truth was often so built upon as to obscure it. "Peter Pindar" was in his element poking fun at George's ignorance, as shown when looking through Lord Pembroke's treasures at Wilton House.

" 'Who's this? Who's this? Who's this fine fellow here?'

'Sesostris,' bowing low, replied the Peer.

'*Sir Sostris*, hey? *Sir Sostris?* 'Pon my word!

Knight or a Baronet, my Lord?

One of *my making?* what, my Lord, *my making?*'

•   •   •   •   •   •   •   •   •

'Pray, pray, my Lord, who's that big fellow there?'

''Tis Hercules,' replied the *shrinking* Peer.

'Strong fellow, hey, my Lord? strong fellow, hey?

Clean'd stables; crack'd a Lion like a flea;

Kill'd Snakes, great Snakes, that in a cradle found him—The

Queen, Queen's coming: wrap an apron round him.' "

The best thing that Wolcot ever wrote, and one that provoked a laugh all over England, was "The King and the Apple-Dumplings," in which he described George's astonishment at first seeing a dumpling, one of which he took into his hand to examine:

" ''Tis monstrous, monstrous hard, indeed,' he cried:

'What makes it, pray, so hard?' The Dame replied,

Low curtseying, 'Please your Majesty, the Apple!'

'Very astonishing indeed! Strange thing!'

(Turning the Dumpling round, rejoined the King).

''Tis most extraordinary then, all this is;

It beats Pinetti's conjuring all to pieces:

Strange I should never of a Dumpling dream!

But, Goody, tell me where, where, where's the seam?'

'Sir, there's no Seam,' quoth she, 'I never knew

That folks did Apple-Dumplings *sew.*'

'No!' said the staring Monarch with a grin:

'How, how the devil got the Apple in?' "

Since it was thought unwise to prosecute Wolcot, after a time an endeavour was made to silence him by gentler means, and, through the instrumentality of Yorke, the Government offered the satirist a pension of three hundred a year, at which he professed to be much astonished:

"Great is the shout indeed, Sir, all abroad,

That you have order'd me this handsome thing;

On which, with lifted eyes, I've said, 'Good God!

Though great my merits, yet how great the King!'

And yet, believe me, Sir, I lately heard

That all your doors were doubly lock'd and barr'd

Against the Poet for his tuneful art;

And that the tall, stiff, stately, red Machines,

Your Grenadiers, the guards of Kings and Queens,

Were ordered all to stab me to the heart:

That if to the House of Buckingham I came,

Commands were given to Mistress Brigg,

A comely, stout, two-handed Dame,

To box my ears and pull my wig;

The Cooks to spit me; curry me, the Grooms;

And Kitchen queans to baste me with their brooms.

You're told that in my ways I'm very evil;

So ugly, fit to travel for a show;

And that I loot all grimly where I go,

Just like a devil;

With horns, and tail, and hoop, that make folks start,

And in my breast a Mill-stone for a Heart."

Nothing came of the proposal, for it fell through owing to a difference of opinion as to the conditions which it would carry with it.

"This pension was well meant, O glorious King,

And for the Bard a very pretty thing:

But let me, Sir, refuse it, I implore;

I ought not to be rich while you are poor.

No, Sir, I cannot be your humble Hack:

I fear your Majesty would break my back."

Wolcot then made a bid for the favour of the Prince of Wales in the "Expostulatory Odes."

"Elate, to Carlton House my rhymes I sent,

Before the Poem met the public eye:

Which gain'd *applause*, the Poet's great intent

But naught *besides*, I say it with a sigh."

Thereafter, but not necessarily because of this, he found the Prince nearly as useful a subject for his scathing verses as the King, and when the former was appointed Regent, "Peter Pindar" was ready with "The Royal First-Born, or, The Baby out of his Leading Strings."

"The P[rince] he promised to *be good*,

And do as every R[egen]t should,

Nor give vile slander cause to say things:

He owned with grief his conduct *wildish*,

And swore no longer to be *childish*,

But part with his *Imperial Playthings*.

This is the day when Britain's pride

Shall throw his leading-strings aside,

And pass a solemn confirmation;

And, being now arrived at age,

From hence shall for himself engage

To do his duty to the nation.

No longer like a baby toss

The bold M[aho]n as his ball,

Make S[heri]d[a]n his rocking horse,

Himself a laughing stock for all.

When he no more in many a frolic

Shall give to Decency the Cholic,

Hang Truth in his imperial garters,

Butchers good-breeding at a jerk,

And crucify (O Parricide and Turk!)

Poor Virtue and Morality, like Martyrs."

He often returned to administer castigation to the Prince, whose profligacies were notorious, and when the heir-apparent was said to be suffering from a sprained ankle, he voiced the general opinion that the confinement was the result of a thrashing from Lord Yarmouth, whose wife had been insulted by "The First Gentleman of Europe."

"Ye Princes, as you love your lives,

Ne'er meddle with *your neighbours' wives*,

But keep your brittle hearts from tripping;

Lest some rude *Lord*, to scare beholders,

Should compliment your princely shoulders,

With such another *royal* whipping.

So let us sing, Long live the King,

The Regent long live he;

And when again he gets a *sprain*,

May I be there to see."

Wolcot's sight began to fail, and in 1811 he was nearly blind, but he still contrived to continue his literary work almost until his death, which took place on 14th January 1819. By his express desire he was buried in St Paul's Church, Covent Garden, by the side of the coffin which contained the mortal remains of Samuel Butler, of whom, perhaps, and not without some reason, he considered himself a humble disciple.

He was a very sane man, sensible of his limitations, and not given to value his work unduly. Indeed, in his first work, "The Epistle to Reviewers," he stated the position to which he aspired:

"I am no cormorant for Fame, d'ye see;

I ask not *all* the laurel, but a *sprig*:

Then hear me, Guardian of the sacred Tree,

And stick a Leaf or two about my wig."

At the same time, he was by no means inclined to hide his light under a bushel, and his verses contain many deliberately humorous references to his talents. "Had I not stepped forward as the Champion of my own Merit (which is deemed so necessary now-a-days for the obtention of public notice, not only by Authors, but by tête-makers, perfumers, elastic truss and Parliament-speech makers, &c., who, in the daily newspapers, are the heralds of *their own* splendid abilities)," he wrote in "Subjects for Painters," "I might possibly be passed by without observation; and thus a great part of a poetical Immortality be sacrificed to a pitiful *mauvaise honte*."

Of course he made many enemies, as every satirist must, but he bore attacks unflinchingly, as, indeed, every satirist should.

"Great are my Enemies in Trade, God knows:

There's not a Poet but would stop my note;

With such a world of Spite their venom flows,

With such *good-will* the knaves would cut my throat."

As a rule he treated his revilers with good-humoured banter, but once a critic raised his ire by an unmerciful attack on his "Nil Admirari, or, A Smile at a Bishop," in *The Anti-Jacobin*, in which he was styled, "this disgraceful subject, the profligate reviler of his sovereign and impudent blasphemer of his God." Gifford at once issued as a counterblast, "An Epistle to Peter Pindar," the savagery of which made the subject so sore that he endeavoured to thrash the author, who, however, had the best of the struggle.

"False fugitive! back to thy vomit flee—

Troll the lascivious song, the fulsome glee;

Truck praise for lust, hunt infant genius down,

Strip modest merit of its last half-crown;

Blow from thy mildew'd lips, on virtue blow,

And blight the goodness thou canst never know.

•   •   •   •   •   •   •   •

But what is he that with a Mohawk's air,

Cries havock, and lets slip the dogs of war?

A blotted mass, a gross unkneaded clod,

A foe to man, a renegade from God,

From noxious childhood to pernicious age,

Separate to infamy, through every stage."

Yet the man of whom these words were spoken was described by his friends as of "a kind and hearty disposition," with little or no malice in his composition, a lover of flowers, music and art. Not even his blindness or the infirmities of age soured his temper, and in his last years he said to Cyrus Redding, "You have seen something of life in your time. See and learn all you can more. You will fall back upon it when you grow old—an old fool is an inexcusable fool to himself and others—store up all; our acquirements are most useful when we become old." Yet he did not suffer age gladly, and when on his death-bed John Taylor asked, "Is there anything I can do for you?" the reply—Wolcot's last words on earth— came. "Bring me back my youth."

"The historian of *Sir Joseph Banks* and *The Emperor of Morocco*, of the *Pilgrims and the Peas*, of the *Royal Academy*, and of *Mr Whitebread's Brewing-Vat*, the bard in whom the nation and the King delighted," Hazlitt wrote the year before the satirist died, "is old and blind, but still merry and wise; remembering how he has made the world laugh in his time, and not repenting of the mirth he has given; with an involuntary smile lighted up at the mad pranks of his Muse, and the lucky hits of his pen—'faint pictures of those flashes of his spirit, that were wont to set the table in a roar'; like his own expiring taper, bright and fitful to the last; tagging a rhyme or conning his own epitaph; and waiting for the last summons, grateful and contented." Indeed, while the coarseness and offensiveness of many of Wolcot's works must be admitted and deplored, it is impossible not to like the man, for he was such a jovial wight, so well able to appreciate a joke against himself and ready to join in the laugh, a very prince of good fellows in an age of less severe restrictions in taste and morality.

Sterne's Eliza

Not Swift so loved his Stella, Scarron his Maintenon, or Waller his Sacharissa, as I will love, and sing thee, my bride elect! All these names, eminent as they were, shall give place to thine, Eliza." Thus Sterne in a letter to Mrs Elizabeth Draper, written in the early part of the year 1767; and though, in spite of this fervent protestation, not Stella, nor Maintenon, nor Sacharissa has paled before Eliza, yet most assuredly Eliza has come to be ranked with them among the heroines of romance.

Of the antecedents of Mrs Draper nothing apparently was generally known to writers on the subject until 1897, when Mr Thomas Seccombe, in the article in the *Dictionary of National Biography* on William Sclater, Rector of Pitminster, showed that her descent could be traced from William's father, Anthony. Anthony Sclater, born in 1520, was appointed in 1570 Rector of Leighton Buzzard, which benefice he held until his death in 1620, when he was succeeded in this clerical office by a younger son, Christopher. Christopher's son William served in the Civil Wars as a Cornet of Horse, and subsequently entered the Church. He was presented in 1666 to the living of St James's, Clerkenwell, and later became Rector of Hadley. He died in 1690, having outlived by five years his son Francis. Francis had a son Christopher, born in 1679, who held the livings of Loughton and Chingford, in Essex, married in 1707 Elizabeth, daughter of John May, of Working, Hants, and by her had thirteen children. The tenth son, May, born on 29th October 1719, went out to India, probably as a cadet in the service of the East India Company, and there married a Miss Whitehall, who bore him three daughters, Elizabeth (Sterne's Eliza), born on 5th April 1744, Mary, and Louisa. The only other children of Christopher with which this narrative is concerned are Elizabeth, who married Dr Thomas Pickering, Vicar of St Sepulchre's, and Richard, the fourth son, born in 1712, who became an alderman of the City of London.16

When his daughters were born, May Sclater was factor of Anjengo, on the Malabar coast, and it was long assumed that his girls were brought up there. Even so late as 1893, Mr James Douglas, the author of "Bombay and Western India," gave credence to the legend, and after stating that there were very few Europeans at Anjengo, "it seems a marvel," he added, "how, never having been in Europe, Eliza should yet have been able to carry herself and attract so much attention there from men who, whatever were their morals, claimed a first position in society and letters." However, as a matter of fact, like most children born in India of English parents, Eliza and her sisters were at an early age sent home for the sake of their health.

In England Eliza stayed alternately with her aunt, Mrs Pickering, and with her uncle, Richard, for whose eldest children, Thomas Mathew and Elizabeth, she conceived an enduring affection. Not until she was in her fourteenth year did she return to her father, now a widower, and she arrived two days after Christmas, 1757, at Bombay, where he then resided.

"I was never half so much rejoiced at going to any ball in my life as when we first saw the land," (she wrote to her cousin in England, Elizabeth Sclater, 13th March 1758). "The Dutch people are white, but their servants are all black, they wear nothing at all about them but a little piece of rag about their waist which to us at first appeared very shocking."

"My Papa's house is the best in Bombay, and where a great deal of company comes every day after dinner."

Among the company that came to May Sclater's house was Daniel Draper, who, entering the East India Company's service in or about 1749, had in the intervening nine years risen to a fairly good position. In those days lads went out to India at an early age, and Draper, in 1757, may well have been no more than thirty, though Dr Sidney Lee has suggested that he was at least four years older. Draper fell in love with Eliza, and married her on 28th July 1758, she being then but fourteen. Such marriages, however, were not then uncommon in India. Two children were born of this union, a boy in 1759, and a girl in October 1761.

Mrs Draper suffered from ill-health, and in 1765, with her husband and children, she came to England. The children were taken to an establishment at Enfield, where Anglo-Indian children were cared for during the absence of their parents in the tropical zone, and presently Draper had to return to his post in Bombay. Mrs Draper, however, remained in England to recover her strength. She stayed with relatives of her mother and father, but with her movements we are not here concerned until she was temporarily domiciled in London during the winter of 1766. It was not until December of that year that she met Sterne, probably at the town house in Gerrard Street, Soho, of William James and his wife—the "Mr and Mrs J." of Sterne's published correspondence.

William James, Commodore of the Bombay Marine, having amassed a fortune by prize-money and mercantile enterprises, retired from the service at the age of eight and thirty, and came to England in 1759, when he purchased an estate at Eltham, near Blackheath, and married Anne, daughter of Edmund Goddard, of Hartham, in Wiltshire. Presently he became chairman of the East India Company, and in 1778, five years before his death, he was made a baronet. When Sterne first became acquainted with the Jameses cannot now be determined, but probably it was not earlier than after his return from the second visit to the Continent.

It is evident, however, that he was on very intimate terms with them at the end of 1766, as his references to them in his letters to Mrs Draper show, though they are mentioned for the first time to his daughter, then with her mother at Marseilles, in a letter dated 23rd February 1767. In this letter we learn that the gossips were already busy coupling Sterne's name with Mrs Draper's.

"I do not wish to know who was the busy fool, who made your mother uneasy about Mrs Draper. 'Tis true I have a friendship for her, but not to infatuation—I believe I have judgment enough to discern hers, and every woman's faults. I honour thy mother for her answer—'that she wished not to be informed, and begged him to drop the subject.'"

Nor was Mrs Sterne's informant the only person who disapproved of the relations of Sterne and Mrs Draper.

"The ——'s, by heavens, are worthless! I have heard enough to tremble at the articulation of the name.—How could you, Eliza, leave them (or suffer them to leave you, rather), with impressions the least favourable? I have told thee enough to plant disgust against their treachery to thee, to the last hour of thy life! Yet still, thou toldest Mrs James at last, that thou believest they affectionately love thee.—Her delicacy to my Eliza, and true regard to her ease of mind, have saved thee from hearing more glaring proofs of their baseness.—For God's sake write not to them; nor foul thy fair character with such polluted hearts. *They* love thee! What proof? Is it their actions that say so? or their zeal for those attachments, which do thee honour, and make thee happy? or their tenderness for thy fame? No.—But they *weep*, and say *tender things.*—Adieu to such for ever. Mrs James's honest heart revolts against the idea of ever returning them one visit. I honour her, and I honour thee, for almost every act of thy life, but this blind partiality for an unworthy being."

The remonstrances of these friends of Eliza were not so outrageous as Sterne deemed them. There was, indeed, some ground for gossip, though perhaps not for scandal—enough, certainly, to alarm people interested in the lady: Sterne's visits to Mrs Draper were too frequent, and Mrs Draper was so indiscreet as to visit Sterne at his lodgings in Old Bond Street and dine there with him *tête-à-tête*. There has been much discussion as to whether the relations of the Brahmin and the Brahmine, as they loved to call each other, were innocent or guilty; but there can be no doubt that the intimacy was not carried to the last extreme. "I have had no commerce whatever with the sex—not even with my wife—these fifteen years," Sterne told his physicians shortly after Eliza had returned to India. This in itself would not be conclusive evidence, though there could have been no reason for him to lie to these people; but the fact that he wrote down this conversation in a Journal intended exclusively for the eye of Mrs Draper makes it certain that his assertion was accurate—at least, so far as he and she were concerned. A man would scarcely trouble falsely to tell his mistress in confidence that he had had no intimacy with her. The Jameses most certainly believed in the innocence of the friendship, else they could scarcely have countenanced it; and not even Thackeray, who shares with John Croft the distinction of being Sterne's most envenomed critic, could have believed that the following letter (whether ultimately despatched or not) could have been written by a guilty man.

LAURENCE STERNE TO DANIEL DRAPER

"Sir, I own it, Sir, that the writing a Letter to a gentleman I have not the honour to be known to, and a Letter likewise upon no kind of business (in the Ideas of the World) is a little out of the common course of Things— but I'm so myself—and the Impulse which makes me take up my pen is out of the Common way too—for it arises from the honest pain I should feel in avowing in so great esteem and friendship as I bear Mrs Draper—If I did not wish and hope to extend it to Mr Draper also. I fell in Love with your Wife—but 'tis a Love you would honour me for—for 'tis so like that I bear my own daughter who is a good creature, that I scarce distinguish a difference betwixt it—the moment I had—that Moment would have been the last. I wish it had been in my power to have been of true use to Mrs Draper at this Distance from her best Protector—I have bestowed a great deal of pains (or rather I should say pleasure) upon her head—her heart needs none—and her head as little as any Daughter of Eve's—and indeed less than any it has been my fate to converse with for some years.—I wish I could make myself of any Service to Mrs Draper whilst she is in India—and I in the world—for worldly affairs I could be of none.—I wish you, dear Sir, many years' happiness. 'Tis a part of my Litany to pray for her health and Life—She is too good to be lost—and I would out of pure zeal take a pilgrimage to Mecca to seek a Medicine."17

If the intimacy was, as is here contended, not carried to the last extreme, there is no doubt of the vigour with which Sterne and his Brahmine flirted, and therefore Sterne cannot be acquitted of insincerity when he wrote to Daniel Draper that he looked upon Eliza as a daughter. But if there is little that is paternal in the few letters of his to Mrs Draper that have been preserved, on the other hand there is nothing from which the conclusion of undue intimacy can be built up.

It may be taken for granted that Mrs Draper's feelings were not very deeply engaged by Sterne. A woman of three and twenty does not often find such enduring attraction in a man of four and fifty as a man of that age does in a woman more than thirty years his junior. But Sterne had fame and undoubted powers of fascination, and Mrs Draper had in her composition an innocent vanity that induced her to encourage him. The homage of one of the most famous men in England was a compliment not lightly to be ignored; and, being flattered, Eliza, unhappy at home, was far from unwilling to enjoy herself abroad. She was clever and bright—perhaps a little bitter, too, remembering that she had been married before she was old enough to know what marriage meant, to a man with uncongenial tastes, dour, and bad-tempered. It is to her credit that she never told Sterne of her marital infelicity, though candid friends left him in no doubt as to her relations with her husband. "Mrs James sunk my heart with an infamous account of Draper and his detested character," Sterne wrote in the "Journal to Eliza" on 17th April 1767, a few weeks after the lady to whom it was addressed had sailed for India.

Eliza is a figure so fascinating to the world interested in the personal side of literary history that a few pages may perhaps be devoted to tracing her life after her acquaintance with Sterne. She was undoubtedly an attractive woman, and made conquest of others than the author of "Tristram Shandy" during this visit to England. The Abbé Raynal, a man about the same age as Sterne, fell a victim to her charms, and expressed his passion in a strange and wild piece of bombast, which he inserted in the second edition of his "History of the Indies."

It was not only to men of middle age that Mrs Draper appealed, for her cousin and playmate of her youth, Thomas Mathew Sclater, was one of her most devoted admirers. That she was fascinating may be taken for granted, but wherein lay her attractiveness is not so clear. Raynal laid more stress on the qualities of her mind than on her appearance. Sterne, too, by his own not too artless confession, was in the first instance drawn to her by something other than her good looks.

"I have just returned from our dear Mrs James's, where I have been talking of thee for three hours" (he wrote to her when they had become well acquainted). "She has got your picture, and likes it; but Marriot, and some other judges, agree that mine is the better, and expressive of a sweeter character. But what is that to the original? yet I acknowledge that hers is a picture for the world, and mine is calculated only to please a very sincere friend, or sentimental philosopher.—In the one, you are dressed in smiles, and with all the advantage of silks, pearls, and ermine;—in the other, simple as a vestal—appearing the good girl nature made you: which, to me, conveys an idea of more unaffected sweetness, than Mrs Draper, habited for conquest, in a birthday suit, with her countenance animated, and her dimples visible.—If I remember right, Eliza, you endeavoured to collect every charm of your person into your face, with more than *common* care, the day you sat for Mrs James.—Your colour, too, brightened; and your eyes shone with more than usual brilliancy. I then requested you to come simple and unadorned when you sat for me—knowing (as I see with *unprejudiced* eyes) that you could receive no addition from the silk-worm's aid, or jeweller's polish. Let me now tell you a truth, which, I believe, I have uttered before. When I first saw you, I beheld you as an object of compassion, and as a very plain woman. The mode of your dress (though fashionable) disfigured you. But nothing now could render you such, but the being solicitous to make yourself admired as a handsome one.—You are not handsome, Eliza, nor is yours a face that will please the tenth part of your beholders—but are something more; for I scruple not to tell you, I never saw so intelligent, so animated, so good a countenance; nor was there (nor ever will be) that man of sense, tenderness, and feeling, in your company three hours, that was not (or will not be) your admirer, or friend, in consequence of it; that is, if you assume, or assumed, no character foreign to your own, but appeared the artless being nature designed you for. A something in your eyes, and voice, you possess in a degree more persuasive than any woman I ever saw, read, or heard of. But it is that bewitching sort of nameless excellence that men of nice sensibility alone can be touched with."

While all are agreed that Mrs Draper had beauty of expression rather than perfectly formed features, there was given a description of her as having "an appearance of artless innocence, a transparent complexion, consequent upon delicate health, but without any sallowness, brilliant eyes, a melodious voice, an intellectual countenance, unusually lighted up with much animation and expressing a sweet gentleness of disposition."18 She had, we are told, engaging manners and numerous accomplishments. She talked well and wrote well, and could play the piano and the guitar. Her faults were a tendency to pecuniary extravagance and a liking for admiration— which latter trait, in her correspondence, she admitted and bewailed. She was also, it must be admitted, a most arrant flirt.

MRS DRAPER TO HER COUSIN, THOMAS MATHEW SCLATER

"*Earl Chatham*, May 2nd, 1767.
(OFF SANTIAGO.   )

". . . From the vilest spot of earth I ever saw, and inhabited by the ugliest of Beings—I greet my beloved cousin—St Jago the place—a charming passage to it—fair winds and fine weather all the way. Health, too, my friend, is once more returned to her enthusiastic votary. I am all Life, air, and spirits—who'd have thought it—considering me in the light of an Exile. And how do you, my Sclater?—and how sat the thoughts of my departure on your Eyes? and how the reality of it? I want you to answer me a thousand questions, yet hope not for an answer to them for many, many months. I am. . . . Did you receive a letter I wrote you from the Downs, with a copy of one enclosed from Sterne to me with his sermons and 'Shandy'? I sent such to you, notwithstanding the Bagatelle airs I give myself—my heart heaves with sighs, and my eyes betray its agitating emotions, every time I think of England and my valuable connections there—ah, my Sclater, I almost wish I had not re-visited that charming country, or that it had been my fate to have resided in it for ever, but in the first instance the Lord's will be done, mine I hope may be accomplished in the second."

MRS DRAPER TO THOMAS MATHEW SCLATER

"*Earl Chatham*, November 29th, 1767.
(OFF THE MALABAR COAST.   )

"They all tell me I'm so improved—nothing—I say to what I was in England—nobody can contradict the assertion—and if it adds to my consequence, you know—it is good policy. Always self to be the subject of your pen (you say) Eliza—why not, my dear cousin? Why have I not as good a right to tell you of my perfections as Montaigne had to divulge to the World he loved white wine better than red? with several other Whims, Capricios, bodily complaints, infirmities of temper, &c., &c.—of the old Gascoignes, not but I love his essays better than most modern ones—and think those that have branded him with the name of Egotist—deserve to be Debar'd the pleasure of speaking of—or looking at themselves—how is it we love to laugh, and yet we do not often approve the person who feeds that voracious passion? Human nature this! vile rogue!—'tis a bad picture—however there's a great resemblance. . . . Once a year is tax enough on a tender Conscience, to sit down premeditatedly to write fibs—and let it not enter your imagination that you are to correspond with me in such terms as your heart dictates. No, my dear Sclater—such a conduct though perfectly innocent (and to me worth all the studied periods of Labour'd Eloquence) would be offensive to my Husband—whose humour I now am resolved to study—and if possible conform to if the most punctilious attention—can render me necessary to his happiness . . . be so—Honour—prudence—and the interest of my beloved children . . . and the necessary Sacrifice—and *I will make it.* Opposing his will will not do—let me now try, if the conforming to it, in every particular will better my condition—it is my wish, Sclater—it is my ambition (indeed it is)—to be more distinguished as a good wife than as the agreeable woman I am in your partial Eyes even—'tis true I have vanity enough to think I have understanding sufficient to give laws to my Family, but as that cannot be, and Providence for wise purposes constituted the male the Head—I will endeavour to act an underpart with grace. 'Where much is given, much is required.' I will think of this proverb and learn humility."

Laurence Sterne

MRS DRAPER TO HER AUNT, MRS PICKERING

"BOMBAY, HIGH MEADOW, *March 21st, 1768.*

"I found my Husband in possession of health, and a good post. Providence will, I hope, continue to him the blessing of the one and the Directors at home, that of the other. My agreeable sister is now a widow, and so much improved in mind and person, as to be a very interesting object. May she be so far conscious of her own worth as to avoid throwing herself away a second time."

MRS DRAPER TO THOMAS MATHEW SCLATER

"TELLICHERY, *May 1769.*

"Mr D. has lost his beneficial post at Bombay, and is, by order of the Company, now Chief in one of the Factories subordinate to it. This was a terrible blow to us at first, but use has in some measure reconciled the mortifying change, though we have no prospect of acquiring such an independence here as will enable us to settle in England for many, very many years, as the country for some time has been the seat of war, and still continues subject to frequent alarms from the growing power of an ambitious usurper. I've no doubt but a general massacre of the English will ensue, if he once more visits this coast. Our fortifications are a wretched burlesque upon such. Troops not better soldiers than trained Bands, and too few in number to cope with so able a general and politician.

"I was within an hour once of being his prisoner, and cannot say but I thought it a piece of good fortune to escape that honour, though he has promised to treat all English ladies well that cheerfully submit to the laws of his seraglio. The way of life I'm now in is quite new to me, but not utterly unpleasant. I'm by turns the wife of a Merchant, Soldier, and Innkeeper, for in such different capacities is the Chief of Tellichery destined to act. The War is a bar to Commerce, yet I do a great deal of business in the mercantile way, as my husband's amanuensis. You know his inability to use the pen, and as he has lost his Clerks and Accountant, without any prospect of acquiring others, I'm necessitated to pass the greatest part of my time in his office, and consent to do so, as it gives me consequence and him pleasure. I really should not be unhappy here if the Motive for which we left England could be as easily accomplished as at Bombay, but that cannot be without an advantageous place—then indeed we should do very well.

"The country is pleasant and healthy (a second Montpelier), our house (a fort and property of the Company) a magnificent one, furnished, too, at our Master's expense, and the allowance for supporting it creditably, what you would term genteelly, though it does not defray the charge of Liquors, which alone amount to six hundred a year, and such a sum, vast as it seems, does not seem extravagant in our situation. For we are obliged to keep a public table, and six months in the year have a full house of shipping Gentry, that resort to us for traffic and intelligence from all parts of India, China, and Asia. Our Society at other times is very confined, as it only consists of a few factors, and two or three families: and such we cannot expect great intercourse with on account of the heavy rains and terrible thunder with lightning to which this Coast is peculiarly subject six months in the year. . . . I flatter myself I'm beloved by such of the Malabars as are within reach of my notice. I was born upon their coast, which is an argument in my favour. . . . I never go out without a guard of six Sepoys (Mahomedan soldiers) armed with drawn sabres and loaded pistols, as some of the natives are treacherous and might be induced to insult a woman of *my Consequence* without a Veil."

MRS DRAPER TO THOMAS MATHEW SCLATER

"SURAT, *April 5th, 1771.*

". . . I received your affectionate letter, my dear Coz, and I prophecy that I shall answer it very stupidly for I danced last night—supped on a cool terrace, and sat up till three o'clock this morning. This may appear nothing very extraordinary to you, my spirits and love of the graceful movement considered, but it was a very great undertaking, the climate, my plan of temperance and exercise considered; for you must know that I find it necessary to live simply mechanical, in order to preserve the remains of a broken constitution and some traces of my former appearance. I rise with the lark daily, and as constantly amble some eight or sixteen miles—after the fox too, occasionally, but field sports have something Royal with them here. What think you of hunting the Antelope with Leopards? This I have frequently done, and a noble diversion it is. Early hours and abstemious Diet are absolutely necessary to the possession of health in India, and I generally conform to the one, and invariably practise the other. Ten or eleven o'clock at the latest, is the usual time of retiring, and soup or vegetables with sherbet and milk constitutes the whole of my regimen. Still I cannot acquire anything like confirmed health or strength here; but if this mode of living preserves my being, my cheerfulness and natural disposition to make the best of things will I hope teach me to bear it. . . . At least I will not thro' any fault of my own, return to Europe with the dregs of life only, but endeavour by every honest means to preserve such a position of animating spirit as may qualify me for the character of an agreeable companion; and then, who knows but cool weather, fashionable society and the animating presence of those I love may enable me

'Formed by their converse happily to steer
From grave to gay, from lively to severe.'

"Do you know that I begin to think all praise foreign but that of true desert. It was not always so, but this same solitude produces reflection, and reflection is good.

"It is an enemy to everything that is not founded on truth, consequently I grow fond of my own approbation and endeavour to deserve it by such a mode of thinking and acting as may enable me to acquire it. Seriously, my dear Sclater, I believe I shall one day be a good moralist."

MRS DRAPER TO MRS RICHARD SCLATER

"BOMBAY, *February 6th, 1772.*

"I cannot say that we have any immediate hopes of returning to England as independent people. India is not what it was, my dear Madam, nor is even a moderate fortune to be acquired here, without more assiduity and time than the generality of English persons can be induced to believe or think of as absolutely necessary; but this Idea, painful as it is to many adventurers who've no notion of the difficulties they are to encounter in the road to wealth, would not affect me considerably, if I had not some very material reasons for wishing to leave the Climate expeditiously. My health is much prejudiced by a Residence in it, my affection for an only child, strongly induces me to bid farewell to it before it is too late to benefit by a change of scene. Mr Draper will in all probability be obliged to continue here some years longer, but, as to myself, I hope to be permitted to call myself an inhabitant of your country before I am two years older."

MRS DRAPER TO MRS ANNE JAMES

"BOMBAY, *April 15th, 1772.*

"You wonder, my dear, at my writing to Becket—I'll tell you why I did so. I have heard some Anecdotes extremely disadvantageous to the Characters of the Widow and Daughter [of Sterne], and that from Persons who said they had been personally acquainted with them, both in France and England. . . . Some part of their Intelligence corroborated what I had a thousand times heard from the Lips of Yorick, almost invariably repeated. . . . The Secret of my Letters being in her hands, had somehow become extremely Public: it was noticed to me by almost every Acquaintance I had in the Ships, or at this Settlement—this alarmed me, for at that time I had never communicated the circumstance and could not suspect you of acting by me in any manner which I would not have acted in by myself—One Gentleman in particular told me that both you and I should be deceived, if we had the least reliance on the Honor or Principles of Mrs Sterne, for that, when she had secured as much as she could for suppressing the Correspondence she was capable of selling it to a Bookseller afterwards—by either refusing to return it to you—or taking Copies of it, without our knowledge—and therefore He advised me, if I was averse to its Publication, to take every means in my Power of Suppressing it—this influenced me to write to Becket and promise Him a reward equal to his Expectations if He would deliver the letters to you. . . .

"My dear Friend, that stiffness you complain'd of, when I called you Mrs James I said I could not accost you with my usual Freedom entirely arose from a Depression of Spirits, too natural to the mortified, when severe Disappointments gall the Sense—You had told me that Sterne was no more—I had heard it before, but this Confirmation of it truly afflicted me; for I was almost an Idolator of his Worth, while I found Him the Mild, Generous, Good Yorick, We had so often thought Him to be—to add to my regret for his loss his Widow had my letters in her Power (I never entertained a good opinion of her), and meant to subject me to Disgrace and Inconvenience by the Publication of them. You know not the contents of these letters, and it was natural for you to form the worst judgment of them, when those who had seen 'em reported them unfavourably, and were disposed to dislike me on that Account. My dear girl! had I not cause to feel humbled so Circumstanced—and can you wonder at my sensations communicating themselves to my Pen?

"Miss Sterne's did indeed, my dear, give me a great deal of pain—it was such a one as I by no means deserved in answer to one written in the true Spirit of kindness, however it might have been constructed.—Mr Sterne had repeatedly told me, that his Daughter was as well acquainted with my Character as he was with my Appearance—in all his letters wrote since my leaving England this Circumstance is much dwelt upon. Another, too, that of Mrs Sterne being in too precarious a State of Health, to render it possible that she would survive many months. Her violence of temper (indeed, James, I wish not to recriminate or be severe just now) and the hatefulness of her Character, are strongly urged to me, as the Cause of his Indifferent Health, the whole of his Misfortunes, and the Evils that would probably Shorten his Life—the visit Mrs Sterne meditated, some time antecedent to his Death, he most pathetically lamented, as an adventure that would wound his Peace and greatly embarrass his Circumstances—the former on account of the Eye Witness He should be to his Child's Affections having been alienated from Him by the artful Misrepresentations of her Mother under whose Tutorage she had ever been—and the latter, from the Rapacity of her Disposition—for well do I know, says he, 'that the sole Intent of her Visit is to plague and fleece me— had I Money enough, I would buy off this Journey, as I have done several others—but till my Sentimental Work is published I shall not have a single sou more than will Indemnify People for my immediate Expenses.' The receipt of this Intelligence I heard of Yorick's Death. The very first Ship which left us Afterwards, I wrote to Miss Sterne by—and with all the freedom which my Intimacy with her Father and his Communications warranted—I purposely avoided speaking of her Mother, for I knew nothing to her Advantage, and I had heard a great deal to the reverse—so circumstanced—how could I with any kind of Delicacy Mention a Person who was hateful to my departed Friend, when for the sake of that very Friend I wished to confer a kindness on his Daughter—and to enhance the value of it, Solicited her Society and consent to share my Prospects, as the highest Favor which could be shown to Myself—indeed, I knew not, but Mrs Sterne, from the Description I had received of her, might be no more—or privately confined, if in Being, owing to a Malady, which I have been told the violence of her temper subjects her to."19

It has been stated by many writers that the cause of the unhappy life led by the Drapers at Bombay was the fault of Sterne, whose insidious flatteries undermined the lady's moral rectitude. This, not to put too fine a point on it, is a conclusion as absurd as it is unwarrantable. Mrs Draper was far too intelligent not to realise that Sterne was a sentimentalist, and not to understand that such allusions as to her being his second wife were, if in bad taste, at least meant to be playful, seeing that he was, and knew he was, standing on the threshold of the valley of the shadow of death. Mrs Draper left her husband six years after she had said farewell to Sterne, not because of the author's influence on her, but because her patience, weakened by a long course of unkind behaviour, was finally outraged by her husband's obvious partiality for her maid, Mrs Leeds. She had long desired to leave Draper, and now a legitimate excuse was furnished, which in the eyes of all unprejudiced persons justified the step.

Draper, who seems to have had some suspicion of her intention, watched her closely, and for a while it was impossible for her to get away. At last she escaped from Mazagon on board a King's cutter, and it was stated that she had eloped with one of her admirers, Sir John Clark. The truth was that she accepted his escort to the house of her uncle, Thomas Whitehall, who lived at Masulipatam.

MRS DRAPER TO THOMAS MATHEW SCLATER

"RAJAHMUNDY, 80 miles from MASULIPATAM,
"*January 20th, 1774* .

". . . I will let you into my present situation. I live entirely with my uncle, and I shall continue to do so to the last hour of my life if he continues to wish it as much as he does at present."

Whether her uncle did not continue to desire her company, or whether she tired of the life, cannot be determined, but later, in the year 1774, Mrs Draper returned to England. There she took up her friendship with the Jameses from the point at which it had been interrupted by her departure seven years earlier for India, and she was soon the centre of a distinguished circle. The publication, in 1775, of some of Sterne's letters to her made her somewhat unpleasantly notorious, and she withdrew from London to the comparative seclusion of Bristol, where she remained until her death, three years later. She was buried in Bristol Cathedral, where a monument, depicting two classical figures bending over a shield, one bearing a torch, the other a dove, was erected in her honour. The shield bore the inscription:

Sacred
To the Memory
of
MRS ELIZA DRAPER,
in whom
Genius and Benevolence
were united.
She died August 3, 1778,
aged 35.

The Demoniacs

'Twas at Jesus College, Cambridge," Sterne wrote in the last year of his life, "I commenced a friendship with Mr H——, which has been most lasting on both sides." This "Mr H——" was the notorious John Hall, who added to his patronymic the name of Stevenson after his marriage in 1739 with an heiress, Anne, daughter of Ambrose Stevenson of Manor House, in the parish of Lanchester, county Durham. Born in 1718, the second son of Joseph Hall, counsellor-at-law of Durham, by his wife, Catherine, eldest daughter of Edward Trotter of Skelton Castle, near Guisborough, John Hall-Stevenson, to call him by the name by which he is best known, went in his eighteenth year to the University, for which, though he did not there distinguish himself, he cherished to the end of his days a sincere regard. "I should recommend Cambridge as a place infinitely preferable to the Temple," he wrote to his eldest grandson, on 17th February 1785, "and particularly on account of the connections you may form with young gentlemen of your own age, of the first rank, men that you must live with hereafter: it is the only time of life to make lasting, honourable, and useful friendships. These advantages were lost to me and blasted by premature marriage, the scantiness of my fortune forced me to vegetate in the country, and precluded me from every laudable pursuit suggested by ambition."

The friendship between Sterne and Hall-Stevenson must have been of rapid growth, as Hall-Stevenson went to Jesus College in June 1835, and Sterne left the University when he took his degree in the following January. Hall-Stevenson has been, no doubt accurately, described as a very precocious lad, with Rabelaisian tastes, and again and again his influence with Sterne has been made an excuse for the humorist's lapses from morality and decency. This, however, is most unfair, for when the young men became acquainted Hall-Stevenson was only seventeen years of age, whereas Sterne was two-and-twenty. Be this as it may, of their intimacy at this time there is no doubt, and tradition tells how they studied together—it would be interesting in the light of subsequent events to know what they studied. They called each other cousin, though the relationship, if any, was most remote. "Cousin Anthony Shandy," Hall-Stevenson in days to come signed himself, and Sterne, in the famous dog-Latin letter written a few months before he died, addressed him: "*mi consobrine, consobrinis meis omnibus carior.*"

Hall-Stevenson remained at Cambridge until 1838, then went abroad for a year, and on his return made the "premature marriage" to which allusion has been made. When he and Sterne met again is a problem not easy to solve. Sterne, writing to Bishop Warburton in June 1760, mentioned that he did not know Hall-Stevenson's handwriting. "From a nineteen years' total interruption of all correspondence with him," he said, "I had forgot his hand." Since Sterne is so precise in giving the number of years, it would seem as if he and his college friend had written to each other until 1741, and that in this year the youthful intimacy, after the manner of its kind, had lapsed. Probably for some years they may have drifted apart, but there is an abundance of evidence to show that long before 1760 they were again on the best terms.

The threads of the college friendship, it has generally been stated, were gathered together when Skelton Castle came into the possession of Hall-Stevenson, who thenceforth resided there. As to when this happened the writers on Sterne only agree in remarking that it was not until after 1745, in which year, after the rebellion, Lawson Trotter, the owner of the castle and a noted Jacobite, fled the country; some say that then the property passed to his sister, Hall-Stevenson's mother, and at her death to her son; others that it passed direct to the nephew as the next in tail. All these statements are inaccurate. Lawson Trotter sold Skelton Castle to Joseph Hall in 1727, and Hall-Stevenson, his elder brother having died in childhood, inherited the estate at the death of his father six years later.

Skelton Castle, which is believed to date back before the Conquest, had been added to, a square tower here, a round tower there, by many of its occupiers, Bruces, Cowpers, Trotters, until, when it came into the hands of Hall-Stevenson, it was a quaint patchwork edifice, erected on a platform supported by two buttressed terraces, which raised it high above the surrounding moat. Hall-Stevenson, amused by the picture presented by its medley of architectural styles, christened it "Crazy Castle," and wrote some humorous verses descriptive of it, well worthy to be preserved, especially as they are almost the only lines from his pen that can be printed in this respectable age:

"There is a Castle in the North,

Seated upon a swampy clay,

At present but of little worth,

In former times it had its day.

This ancient Castle is call'd CRAZY,

Whose mould'ring walks a moat environs,

Which moat goes heavily and lazy,

Like a poor prisoner in irons."

Skelton Castle was at this date more than half ruined, as the owner was at some pains to indicate:

"Many a time I've stood and thought,

Seeing the boat upon this ditch,

It look'd as if it had been brought

For the amusement of a witch,

To sail amongst applauding frogs,

With water-rats, dead cats and dogs.

The boat so leaky is, and old,

That if you're fanciful and merry,

You may conceive, without being told,

That it resembles Charon's wherry.

A turret also you may note,

Its glory vanish'd like a dream,

Transform'd into a pigeon-coat,

Nodding beside the sleepy stream.

From whence, by steps with moss o'ergrown,

You mount upon a terrace high,

Where stands that heavy pile of stone,

Irregular, and all awry.

If many a buttress did not reach

A kind and salutary hand,

Did not encourage and beseech,

The terrace and the house to stand,

Left to themselves, and at a loss,

They'd tumble down into the foss.

Over the Castle hangs a Tow'r,

Threat'ning destruction every hour;

Where owls, and bats, and the jackdaw,

Their vespers and their Sabbath keep,

All night scream horribly, and caw,

And snore all day in horrid sleep.

Oft at the quarrels and the noise

Of scolding maids or idle boys,

Myriads of rooks rise up and fly,

Like legions of damn'd souls,

As black as coals,

That foul and darken all the sky."

Hall-Stevenson was, as has been remarked, a poor man, and could not afford to undertake the task of repairing the vast structure, though once he thought of making an effort to do so. When Sterne heard of this he wrote protesting against any interference with the fine old structure, and seasoned his letter with a touch of worldly wisdom that comes quaintly from him:

"But what art thou meditating with axes and hammers?—'*I know the pride and the naughtiness of thy heart*,' and thou lovest the sweet visions of architraves, friezes and pediments with their tympanums, and thou hast found out a pretence, *à raison de cinq livres sterling* to be laid out in four years, &c. &c. (so as not to be felt, which is always added by the d——l as a bait) to justify thyself unto thyself. It may be very wise to do this—but 'tis wiser to keep one's money in one's pocket, whilst there are wars without and rumours of wars within. St —— advises his disciples to sell both coat and waistcoat—and go rather without shirt or sword, than leave no money in their scrip to go to Jerusalem with. Now those *quatre ans consecutifs*, my dear Anthony, are the most precious morsels in thy *life to come* (in this world), and thou wilt do well to enjoy that morsel without cares, calculations, and curses, and damns, and debts—for as sure as stone is stone, and mortar is mortar, &c., 'twill be one of the many works of thy repentance.—But after all, if the Fates have decreed it, as you and I have some time supposed it on account of your generosity, '*that you are never to be a monied man*,' the decree will be fulfilled whether you adorn your castle and line it with cedar, and paint it within side and without side with vermilion, or not—*et cela étant* (having a bottle of Frontiniac and glass at my right hand) I drink, dear Anthony, to thy health and happiness, and to the final accomplishments of all thy lunary and sublunary projects."

Notwithstanding this sage counsel, Hall-Stevenson called in an architect, presently to be referred to as "Don Pringello," who, to his credit, declined to tamper with the building, and succeeded in inducing the owner to abandon the plan of reconstruction.

Hall-Stevenson from time to time visited London, and made acquaintance with Horace Walpole, and also with Sir Francis Dashwood and John Wilkes, who introduced him to the Monks of Medmenham and also gave him a taste for politics, that afterwards found vent in some satirical verses. Lack of means, however, prevented his taking any considerable part in metropolitan gaieties, and he lived most of his life on his estate, making an occasional stay at Scarborough or some other northern watering-place. At Skelton, as William Hutton phrased it happily, he "kept a full-spread board, and wore down the steps of his cellar." Steeped in Rabelaisian literature, he caught something of the spirit of the books he had perused; and, inspired by the example of the deceased Duke of Wharton and of his friend Dashwood, he gathered round him a body of men with similar tastes, and founded, in imitation of the Hell-fire Club and the Monks of Medmenham, a society which has passed into history as the Demoniacs.

The number of members of this convivial community cannot have been considerable. Hall-Stevenson in "Crazy Tales" gives eleven stories, each supposed to have been told by one of the band, the identity of the narrator being veiled under a nickname; and if this may be accepted as a guide, then there were but eleven Demoniacs in 1862—though, in a later edition, were added, "Old Hewett's Tale," and "Tom of Colesby's Tale." In most cases it has been easy to discover the names of the members. "Anthony" of the "Crazy Tale" was, of course, the host; and "My Cousin" Sterne, though he was also known among the fraternity as "The Blackbird," probably because of his clerical attire, and under this *sobriquet* was made the subject of one of Hall-Stevenson's "Makarony Fables." "Zachary" was Zachary Moore, of Lofthouse, a fashionable man about town, who spent a great fortune in riotous living; though the only story of his extravagance that has been handed down is, that his horses were always shod with silver, and that when a shoe fell off or was loose, he would have it replaced with a new one. He was a jovial fellow, and popular.

"What sober heads hath thou made ache!

How many hath thou kept from nodding!

How many wise ones, for thy sake,

Have flown to thee, and left off plodding."

Thus he was apostrophised by Hall-Stevenson, who subsequently indited an epitaph for him, which while it does much credit to the writer's heart, does less to his head: such a prodigal as Moore was lucky to be presented with an ensigncy.

"Z. M. Esq." (thus runs the epitaph), "A Living Monument, of the Friendship and Generosity of the Great; After an Intimacy of Thirty Years With most of The Great Personages of these Kingdoms, Who did him the Honour to assist him, In the laborious Work, Of getting to the far End of a great Fortune; These his Noble Friends, From Gratitude For the many happy Days and Nights Enjoyed by his means, Exalted him, through their Influence, In the forty-seventh year of his Age, To an Ensigncy; which he actually enjoys at present at Gibraltar."

The "Privy Counsellor" of the "Tales" has been said to be Sir Francis Dashwood, but upon what grounds this statement has been made is not clear: if the assumption is accurate, the "Privy Counsellor" cannot often have attended the gatherings of the brethren, being usually otherwise engaged in London. "Panty," an abbreviation of Pantagruel, is known to have been the Rev. Robert Lascelles, subsequently the incumbent of Gilling, in the West Riding; and "Don Pringello," whose name has not transpired,20 has his niche in "Tristram Shandy," where it is mentioned: "I am this moment in a handsome pavilion built by Pringello upon the banks of the Garonne." Don Pringello also receives honourable mention in a scholium to the Tale inscribed to his name by "Cousin Anthony."

"Don Pringello" (Hall-Stevenson wrote) "was a celebrated Spanish Architect, of unbounded generosity. At his own expense, on the other side of the Pyrenean Mountains, he built many noble castles, both for private people and for the *public*, out of his own funds; he repaired several palaces, situated upon the pleasant banks of that delightful river, the Garonne, in France, and came over on purpose to rebuild CRAZY-CASTLE; but, struck with its venerable remains, he could only be prevailed upon to add a few ornaments, suitable to the stile and taste of the age it was built in."

"Old Hewett" was that eccentric William Hewett, or Hewitt, introduced into "Humphrey Clinker" by Smollett, who prophesied that, "his exit will be as odd as his life has been extravagant." Smollett's anticipation was justified, even before the novel was published, as the author mentions in a footnote. Hewett in 1767, being then over seventy years of age, was attacked by an internal complaint, and, to quote Smollett,

"he resolved to take himself off by abstinence; and this resolution he executed like an ancient Roman. He saw company to the last, cracked his jokes, conversed freely, and entertained his guests with music. On the third day of his fast, he found himself entirely freed from his complaint; but refused taking sustinence. He said the most disagreeable part of the journey was past, and he should be a cursed fool indeed to put about ship when he was just entering the harbour. In these sentiments he persisted, without any marks of affectation; and thus finished his course with such ease and serenity, as would have done honour to the firmest stoic of antiquity."

There are still unaccounted for, "Captain Shadow," "The Student of Law," "The Governor of Txlbury," "The Lxxb," "The Poet," and "Tom of Colesby"; and against these may be placed other frequenters of Skelton Castle—though it is possible some may not have been of the brotherhood. There were Garland, a neighbouring squire; and Scroope, whom Sterne referred to as "Cardinal S." and who was probably a parson; and "G." of the printed letters, whose name in the originals is given as Gilbert. More likely to have been Demoniacs were Hall-Stevenson's younger brother, Colonel George Lawson Hall (who married a daughter of Lord William Manners), and Andrew Irvine, called by his familiars "Paddy Andrews," master of the Grammar School at Kirkleatham. Because Dr Alexander Carlyle met at Harrogate in the company of Hall-Stevenson that Charles Lee who subsequently became a general in the American army, and fought against his countrymen in the War of Independence, Lee has been written down one of the society; but it is improbable he was enrolled, if only because, leaving England in 1751 at the age of twenty, he was not again in his native land before "Crazy Tales" was written, except for a few months in the spring of 1761.

The Demoniacs (and the title may for the nonce be taken to include all the frequenters of Skelton Castle) have been damned by each succeeding writer who has taken them for his subject; but it is extremely doubtful if they were as black as they have been painted. Had they been merely vulgar debauchees, it is inconceivable that Sterne would have let them make the acquaintance, not only of his wife, but also of the young daughter he cherished so tenderly; and it is only one degree less unlikely that they would have won and retained his affectionate regard for a score of years, or that he would have read to them "Tristram Shandy" and have desired their opinion of the various instalments of that work. His letters are full of references to the Demoniacs, and he rarely wrote to "dear Cousin Anthony" without sending greetings to his associates, and expressing the wish that he was with them.

"Greet the Colonel [Hall] in my name, and thank him cordially from me for his many civilities to Madame and Mademoiselle Sterne, who send all due acknowledgments" (he wrote from Toulouse, 12th August 1762; adding in a postscript:) "Oh! how I envy you all at Crazy Castle! I would like to spend a month with you—and should return back again for the vintage. . . . Now farewell—remember me to my beloved Colonel—greet Panty most lovingly on my behalf, and if Mrs C—— and Miss C——, &c. are at G[uisborough], greet them likewise with a holy kiss—So God bless you."

A couple of months later, Sterne, still at Toulouse, addressed Hall-Stevenson:

"If I had nothing to stop me I would engage to set out this morning, and knock at Crazy Castle gates in three days less time—by which time I should find you and the Colonel, Panty, &c. all alone—the season I most wish and like to be with you."

Again and again are allusions to the Crazelites, as Sterne often called them:

"I send all compliments to Sir C. D[ashwoo]d and G——s. I love them from my soul. If G[ilber]t is with you, him also" (he wrote from Coxwold, 4th September 1764; and from Naples, two years later:). "Give my kind services to my friends—especially to the household of faith—my dear Garland—to the worthy Colonel—to Cardinal S[croope], and to my fellow-labourer Pantagruel."

Even in the last year of his life he looked forward to being present at a reunion at the castle: "We shall all meet from the east, and from the south, and (as at the last) be happy together."

Faults the Demoniacs certainly had; but there is no reason to believe, indeed there is not a jot or tittle of evidence to support the suggestion, that they performed the blasphemous rites associated with the more famous institutions that served as their model. Their indulgences were limited to coarse stories and deep potations; which, after all, were regarded as venial sins in the eighteenth century. Even so, of course, it must be admitted they were not fit company for clergymen, and it is a matter for regret that Sterne should have been of the party. Doubtless Laurence told his story of "A Cock and a Bull" with the best of them; but he was no drunkard, and tried to induce Hall-Stevenson to give up the habit of heavy drinking.

"If I was you, quoth Yorick, I would drink more water, Eugenius" (so runs a passage in "Tristram Shandy"). "And, if I was you, Yorick, replied Eugenius, so would I."

On the other hand, several of the Demoniacs were men of intelligence. With all his vices, Dashwood had brains of no mean order; Irvine, the schoolmaster, and a Cambridge D.D., had, at least, some reading; and Lascelles, a keen fisherman, could write verses—not very good verses, it is true—in Latin and English. It is doubtful, however, if he was that Robert Lascelles who in 1811 wrote the "Letters on Sporting," in which he treated of angling, shooting, and coursing; although this rare work has been attributed to him. William Hewett, too, was a cultured man; he had been tutor to the Marquis of Granby, and was a friend of Voltaire. He had a pretty wit. It has been told how being in the Campidoglio at Rome, Hewett, who owned "no religion but that of nature," made up to the bust of Jupiter, and, bowing very low, exclaimed in the Italian language, "I hope, sir, if ever you get your head above water again, you will remember that I paid my respects to you in your adversity." Indeed that carousals at Skelton Castle were confined to the evening is shown by Hall-Stevenson's account of his guest's occupations during the day.

"Some fell to fiddling, some to fluting,

Some to shooting, some to fishing,

Some to pishing and disputing,

Or to computing by wishing.

And in the evening when they met

(To think on't always does me good,)

There never met a jollier sett,

Either before, or since the Flood."

Nor was Hall-Stevenson a mere voluptuary. Even though the critic may have exaggerated who wrote of him: "He could engage in the grave discussions of criticism and literature with superior power; he was qualified to enliven general society with the smile of Horace, the laughter of Cervantes; or he could sit on Fontaine's easy chair, and unbosom his humour to his chosen friends"; yet there is no doubt that he was a good classical scholar, and, for an Englishman, exceptionally well read in the *belles lettres* of Europe, in a day when such knowledge was rare.

"ANTHONY, Lord of CRAZY Castle,

Neither a fisher, nor a shooter,

No man's, but any woman's vassel,

If he could find a way to suit her";

so he wrote himself down; and the description is good so far as it goes. But though "My Cousin Anthony" thus indicates that, unlike Sterne, he has no liking for field sports, he does not mention that he found his pleasure at home in the great library, that was so rich in what Bagehot has described as "old folio learning and the amatory reading of other days." There the owner browsed for hours together, and he wrought better than he knew when he introduced his friend Sterne to the apartment and made him free of it, for there it was that Sterne found in many quaint forgotten volumes much of that strange lore with which the elder Shandy's mind was packed. Dr Carlyle found Hall-Stevenson a "highly-accomplished and well-bred gentleman," and Sterne's opinion of his old college friend is clearly shown not only in his letters but in the character of "Eugenius" in "Tristram Shandy." There must have been virtues in the man who stood for Eugenius, else Sterne, who had as keen an eye for the weaknesses of his fellows as any author that ever lived, would not have immortalised him as the wise, kindly counsellor of Yorick. How tenderly Sterne rallied "Cousin Anthony" upon his hypochondria.

"And so you think this [letter] cursed stupid—but that, my dear H., depends much upon the quotâ horâ of your shabby clock, if the pointer of it is in any quarter between ten in the morning or four in the afternoon—I give it up—or if the day is obscured by dark engendering clouds of either wet or dry weather, I am still lost—but who knows but it be five—and the day as fine a day as ever shone upon the earth since the destruction of Sodom—and peradventure your honour may have got a good hearty dinner to-day, and eat and drink your intellectuals into a placidulish and blandulish amalgama—to bear nonsense, so much for that."

So he wrote from Coxwould in August 1761; and rather more than a year later, when he was at Toulouse, he reverted to the subject:

"I rejoice from my heart, down to my reins, that you have snatched so many happy and sunshiny days out of the hands of the blue devils. If we live to meet and join our forces as heretofore, we will give these gentry a drubbing—and turn them for ever out of their usurped citadel—some legions of them have been put to flight already by your operations this last campaign—and I hope to have a hand in dispersing the remainder the first time my dear cousin sets up his banners again under the square tower."

Once, indeed, Sterne tried to cure his friend. Hall-Stevenson had a great fear of the effect of the east wind upon his health, and he had a weather-cock placed so that he could see it from the window of his room, and he would consult it every morning. When the wind blew from that quarter he would not get up, or, being up, would retire to bed. During one of Sterne's visits to Skelton Castle he bribed a lad to climb up one night and tie the vane to the west; and Hall-Stevenson, after the customary inspection of the weather-cock, joined his guests the next day without any ill effect, although as a matter of fact an east wind was blowing. The trick was subsequently explained; but it is doubtful if it cured the *malade imaginaire.*

Hall-Stevenson was as devoted to Sterne as Sterne to him, and he made agreeable reference to their affection:

"In this retreat, whilom so sweet,

Once *Tristram* and his cousin dwelt,

They talk of *Crazy* when they meet,

As if their tender hearts would melt."

When the first two volumes of "Tristram Shandy" were published, Hall-Stevenson indicted a lyric epistle "To my Cousin Shandy, on his coming to Town," that, through its indecency, brought in its train more annoyance than pleasure to Sterne; and subsequently (in 1768) parodied the style of the book under the title of "A Sentimental Dialogue between two Souls in the Palpable Bodies of an English Lady of Quality and an Irish Gentleman," introduced by a note: "Tristram Shandy presents his compliments to the Gentlemen of Ireland, and begs their acceptance of a Sentimental Offering, as an acknowledgment due to the Country where he was born." A year after Sterne's death Hall-Stevenson, over the signature of "Eugenius," issued a continuation of "A Sentimental Journey," for which he made the following excuse:

"The Editor has compiled this Continuation of his Sentimental Journey, from such motives, and upon such authority, as he flatters himself will form a sufficient apology to his readers for its publication.

"The abrupt manner in which the Second Volume concluded, seemed forcibly to claim a sequel; and doubtless if the author's life had been spared, the world would have received it from his own hand, as he had materials already prepared. The intimacy which subsisted between Mr Sterne and the Editor, gave the latter frequent occasion of hearing him relate the most remarkable incidents of the latter part of his last journey, which made such an impression on him, that he thinks he has retained them so perfectly as to be able to commit them to paper. In doing this, he has endeavoured to imitate his friends stile and manner, but how far he has been successful in this respect, he leaves the reader to determine. The work may now, however, be considered as complete; and the remaining curiosity of the readers of Yorick's Sentimental Journey, will at least be gratified with respect to facts, events, and observations."

The book opens with an apostrophe to his dead friend:

"Delightful Humourist! thine were unaccountable faculties. Thy Muse was the Muse of joy and sorrow,—of sorrow and joy. Thou didst so exquisitely blend fancy with feeling, mirth with misfortune; thy laughter was so laughable; and thy sighs so sad; that—thou never wast, never will be equalled.—Thou hadst the *Key of the Heart*.—Lend it to a Friend.

"O Yorick, hear me! *Half* thy work is left unfinished, and *all* thy spirit is fled.—Send part of it back. Drop one remnant of it to a Friend."

The prayer was not granted. The mantle of Yorick did not fall upon Eugenius, who had neither the power of humour or pathos, but only the indelicacy a hundredfold increased, of the great man. Indeed, the writings of Hall-Stevenson rendered poor service to his friends, for it was their publication that brought about the forcible condemnation of the Demoniacs: the flagrant indecency of "Crazy Tales" being accepted as a clue to the thoughts and actions of the members of the society. Yet of that little production, which appeared in 1762, the author thought very highly.

"As long as CRAZY Castle lasts,

Their Tales will never be forgot,

And CRAZY may stand many blasts,

And better Castles go to pot."

Thus Hall-Stevenson in his Prologue, doubtless reflecting that since Skelton Castle had endured through seven centuries, it might well brave the breeze for many generations to come. His prophecy was not falsified, for "Crazy Tales" were not forgot until the Castle went to pot—which event, however, took place three years after his death, when his grandson substituted for the unique and picturesque structure a house in which it was possible to live in comfort. Nay, the "Tales" outlived the Castle, being reprinted in 1796, and again four and twenty years later, when they were assigned on the title-page to Sheridan. A glance at the catalogue of the British Museum Library shows that some singularly ill-advised person thought fit in 1896 to reissue the book for private circulation.

That Sterne should find a word of praise for "Crazy Tales" was but natural:

"I honour the man who has given the world an idea of our parental seat— 'tis well done—I look at it ten times a day with a *quando te aspiciam*" (he wrote to his friend from Toulouse soon after the publication of the volume; adding), "I felicitate you upon what messr. the Reviewers allow you—they have too much judgment themselves not to allow you what you are actually possessed of, 'talents, wit, and humour.'—Well, write on, my dear cousin, and be guided by thy fancy."

It is more surprising to find Horace Walpole enlisting himself among Hall-Stevenson's admirers. "They entertained me extremely," he wrote to a friend, returning some verses, "as Mr Hall's works always do. He has a vast deal of original humour and wit, and nobody admires him more than I do. . . . If all authors had as much parts and good sense as he has, I should not be so sick of them as I am." The critics as a body were not so kind, and incurred the resentment of the author, who lashed them in "Two Lyric Epistles," which Gray, writing to the Rev. James Brown,thought "seemed to be absolute madness." The works, which were collected in 1795, were declared by Sir Walter Scott to be witty; but even that tribute has since been denied them. Bagehot dismissed them as having "licence without humour, and vice without amusement," and Whitwell Elwin, in his masterly essay on Sterne, stigmatised the "Crazy Tales" as infamous.

William Beckford of Fonthill Abbey

It may be said with truth that there were few famous men born in the eighteenth century of whom less is known than of William Beckford of Fonthill, the author of "Vathek." There is an abundance of legend, as little trustworthy as most legends, but of the man as he was few people have even a remote conception. This may be partly because there has been no biography of him worthy of the name; but it is, probably, due even more largely to the fact that he led a secluded life. It is certain that stories concerning him, invariably defamatory and usually libellous, were circulated so far back as the days of his minority; and that these were revived when, after his Continental tours, he settled at Fonthill. Then the air of mystery that enveloped him created grave suspicion in the minds of his fox-hunting neighbours. Everything he said was misrepresented and regarded as evidence against him, until so strong was the feeling that it was looked upon by his country neighbours as disgraceful to visit him. This, however, did not prevent Nelson or Sam Rogers or Sir William Hamilton from going to Fonthill, nor, later, did it prevent his acquaintance with Benjamin Disraeli. Notwithstanding, Beckford was accused of almost every conceivable crime, and John Mitford, in one of his unpublished note-books, solemnly recorded that Beckford was accused of poisoning his wife at Cintra. There was no more truth in any other accusation than in this of causing the death of a woman to whom he was deeply attached and whose loss he sincerely mourned. Thirty years after her death, Rogers noticed that there were tears in Beckford's eyes while he was talking of her.

This, however, was but one of many slanders. It was said that Beckford built the high wall round his estate of Fonthill that his orgies might be carried on unperceived—the wall was built because no mere request would keep the hunters off his land, and he could not bear to see the death agonies of a fox. It was said that he kept a number of dwarfs, and with their aid performed blasphemous rites and indulged in magical incantations—he had in his service one dwarf, Piero, whom he had rescued in some Italian town from a cruel father. Even so recently as nine years ago an anonymous writer thought it worth while to record in a literary journal the reminiscences of an elderly lady, who lived at Bath when Beckford resided in that city, who was a child then, and who had no acquaintance with him. This elderly lady stated that "a species of paroxysm would seize Beckford if he saw a woman"—yet a line before she speaks of his riding through the streets of Bath! Were the women of Bath on these occasions, it is legitimate to ask, commanded, like the inhabitants of Coventry when Lady Godiva took her famous airing, to keep out of sight? or was Beckford seen to have paroxysm after paroxysm as his horse took him through the narrow streets of the quaint old city? The same authority relates that at Beckford's house in Lansdown Crescent (Bath) niches were constructed in the walls of the staircase, so that the female servants could conceal themselves when they heard their master's footsteps; and that one girl, to satisfy her curiosity as to what Beckford would do if he saw her, had her curiosity fully satisfied, for the "woman-hater, in a paroxysm of fury, seized her by the waist and threw her over the banisters." This suggests a new version of the Peeping Tom episode, and also brings to mind the nursery rhyme,

"He took her by the left leg and threw her down the stairs."

It is pleasant to be told that the misogynist generously bestowed on the injured maid a pension for life. The story is nearly as good, and doubtless quite as true, as that of the gentleman who killed a waiter at an inn and told the landlord, who thought he must send for the police, to charge it in the bill.

The fact is that the majority of writers on Beckford have been willing to recount what they have heard, without making any attempt at verification, even when such a task would not have been difficult. Beckford, we are told, was as likely to thrash a beggar in the streets as to give him alms. This is really the most truthful of all the charges brought against him, for it actually has for its foundation the fact that he once did strike a beggar! Here is the story: When Beckford was riding one day to Weston, a suburb of Bath, a man near his gates begged from him and received a coin; delighted with his success, the beggar watched which way the donor was going, took a short cut, and at another place again asked for alms, only to be recognised and struck with a whip.

The calumnies that pursued Beckford during his life, and his memory since his death, were bad enough, but the excuses that are made for him nowadays are worse. The writer already referred to as retailing the elderly lady's gossip, unable to account for Beckford's mysterious seclusion and other peculiarities, fell back upon the convenient suggestion of "a mental derangement." "We learn," he said, in support of his contention, "that at his death he showed scarcely a sign of age, a peculiarity frequently noticed, of course, among those with similar mental aberrations." Another peculiarity frequently noticed, among those with similar mental aberrations, we may add, is that at their death many show every sign of age.

William Beckford

Many of those who do not suggest that Beckford was mad love to dwell upon his eccentricities; but an examination of their arguments shows that these eccentricities were limited to the building of Fonthill and a love of seclusion. His seclusion has been vastly exaggerated, and Fonthill was but the whim of a millionaire—a whim, moreover, prompted by a laudable desire to provide employment for the poor of the countryside. What a genius he had "Vathek" proves conclusively; how sane he was to the end of his days may be discerned from the letters written in the last years, even in the last month, of his long life.

The keynote of Beckford's character was enthusiasm. If he undertook anything it must be done forthwith; if he had a desire, he must satisfy it with the least possible delay. Thus, when he built Fonthill he had five hundred men working day and night; when he collected books, he did so with such vigour that in a few years he brought together one of the finest private libraries in the world. That last passion never deserted him, and in his eighty-fourth year he studied catalogues as keenly, and was as impatient for news as to the success that had attended his agent, as when he began half-a-century earlier. Like most men he did not suffer bores gladly, but, unlike the majority, he would not have aught to do with them. Having a genius and a million, he lived his life as he pleased; while welcoming his friends, and opening wide his doors to distinguished writers, artists and musicians, he held the rest of the world at bay, and spent his days with his books and pictures, playing the piano, and superintending his gardens. So well did he order his life that when in his eighty-fifth year the flame was burning out, he could say truthfully, "I have never known a moment's *ennui*."

Beckford was born with a silver spoon in his mouth. Wealth came to him from his father, the Alderman, and aristocratic connections from his mother, the daughter and co-heir of the Hon. George Hamilton, second surviving son of the Sixth Earl of Abercorn. Lord Chatham was his godfather, and when the Alderman died in 1770, not only did Lord Chatham, but also "the good Lord Lyttelton" and Lord Camden, interest themselves in the education of the ten-years-old lad, who, if he lived to attain his majority, would be the wealthiest commoner in England. The Rev. John Lettice was his tutor; Sir William Chambers, who was then rebuilding Somerset House, taught him architecture; and he studied music under Mozart. He learnt declamation, too, and at an early age won the approval of his godfather by reciting with correct emphasis a passage from Thucydides which he had previously translated into English. "May you," the aged statesman said to his son William, "some day make as brilliant a speaker." The cynical may trace from this remark the dislike that subsequently existed between the younger Pitt and Beckford.

"Great pains were bestowed upon my education," Beckford said in his old age. "I was living amidst a fine collection of works of art, under competent tutors. I was studious and diligent from inclination. I was fond of reading whatever came in my way. After my classical studies were finished, and while I worked hard at Persian, I read French and English biographies of all sorts." How much he profited by his education, and how well he remembered what he read, is shown conclusively by the numerous allusions to men and books in the letters written when he was still a lad. He seems, indeed, to have been taught, or to have acquired by reading, some knowledge of most subjects, except, as he subsequently admitted regretfully, astronomy. Like most boys, he preferred the subjects of his own choosing to those he was compelled to study. A chance discussion as to whether the Abercorn branch of the Hamilton family from which his mother was descended was older than the ducal branch sent him early to books of genealogy, and his reading in this byway of history imbued him with a pride of race that nothing could eradicate. His father's ancestry did not satisfy him, and he studied the pedigree of his mother, and declared he could trace it to John of Gaunt. He claimed the distinction of being descended from all the barons (of whom any issue remained) who signed Magna Charta. At a very early age he came across a copy of "The Arabian Nights"—and this chance find had more effect upon his life and character than any other incident. He read and re-read these stories with avidity, and the impression they made on him was so strong that Lord Chatham instructed Lettice that the book must be kept from the boy. The precaution came too late, for, though the injunction was obeyed and for some years "The Arabian Nights" was withheld from him, the Oriental tales had taken possession of the impressionable reader to such an extent that he could never forget them. They had fired his youthful mind and held his imagination captive; their influence over him never waned all the days of his life; and while they inspired him with the idea of "Vathek," they also fostered in him the love of magnificence, inherited from his father, that resulted in the erection of Fonthill Abbey and other extravagances. As a lad, owing to the hold the stories had over him, he became a dreamer and lived in an unreal world; and it is not surprising, therefore, that, though of an amiable disposition, he became wilful and capricious. "Little Beckford was really disappointed at not being in time to see you—a good mark for my young *vivid* friend," Lord Chatham wrote to William Pitt, 9th October 1773. "He is just as much compounded of the elements of *air and fire* as he was. A due proportion of *terrestrial* solidity will, I trust, come and make him perfect."

A boy of thirteen who is all "air and fire" is certain to be spoilt by a doting mother and made much of by visitors to the house, and Beckford's wit was so much encouraged by almost all of them that, in spite of Lettice's admonitions, he frequently got out of hand. Only his relative, the old Duchess of Queensberry—Gay's Duchess—who lived in the neighbourhood, ventured to rebuke him: when he treated her with some lack of respect at her house, without making any reply, she sent a servant for the great family Bible, and made the boy read a passage from the Book of Solomon: "There it was, young man, that I learnt *my* manners," she said impressively; "I hope you will remember what you have read."

Mrs Beckford had refused to allow her son to go to school, and she objected as strongly to send him to a university, regarding the temptations that would there be held out to a young man of enormous wealth as more than counterbalancing the advantages. Eventually it was decided that the lad, now in his seventeenth year, should stay with his relatives, Colonel and Miss Hamilton, who lived at Geneva. Though for the first time emancipated from maternal control, Beckford, happy in his daydreams, showed no desire to kick over the traces. It was at this time that Beckford first gave expression to his intention to adopt a mode of life different from that led by most fashionable young men.

"To receive Visits and to return them, to be mighty civil, well-bred, quiet, prettily Dressed, and smart is to be what your old Ladies call in England a charming Gentleman, and what those of the same stamps abroad know by the appellation of *un homme comme il faut*. Such an Animal how often am I doomed to be" (he wrote at the age of seventeen, in a letter hitherto unpublished). "To pay and to receive fulsome Compliments from the Learned, to talk with modesty and precision, to sport an opinion gracefully, to adore Buffon and d'Alembert, to delight in Mathematics, logick, Geometry, and the rule of Right, the *mal morale* and the *mal physique*, to despise poetry and venerable Antiquity, murder Taste, abhor imagination, detest all the charms of Eloquence unless capable of mathematical Demonstration, and more than all, to be vigorously incredulous, is to gain the reputation of good sound Sense. Such an Animal I am sometimes doomed to be. To glory in Horses, to know how to knock up and how to cure them, to smell of the stable, swear, talk bawdy, eat roast beef, drink, speak bad French, go to Lyons, and come back again with manly disorders, are qualifications not despicable in the Eyes of the English here. Such an Animal I am determined not to be."

After a year and a half's absence Beckford was summoned to England, where he stayed for some months, visiting various cities and country houses, and composing his first book, "Biographical Memoirs of Extraordinary Painters." It was well in keeping with the curious contradictions of Beckford's character, that, while his letters before and after, and even while he was engaged upon the "Memoirs," were so full of dreams, this work should be an amusing burlesque. "I will explain the origin of the 'Memoirs,'" Beckford said to Cyrus Redding in 1835, fifty-five years after its publication. "The housekeeper at old Fonthill, as is customary, used to get her fee by exhibiting the pictures to those who came to see the building. Once or twice I heard her give the most extraordinary names to different artists. I wondered how such nonsense could enter the brain of woman. More than this, in her conceit she would at times expatiate upon excellencies of which the picture before her had no trace. The temptation was irresistible in my humour. I was but seventeen. My pen was quickly in hand composing the 'Memoirs.' In future the housekeeper had a printed guide in aid of her descriptions. She caught up my phrases; the fictitious names of the wives, too, whom I had given to my imaginary painters, were soon learned in addition; her descriptions became more picturesque, her language more graphic than ever, to the sight-seeing people. Mine was the text-book, whoever exhibited the paintings. The book was soon on the tongues of all the domestics. Many were the quotations current upon the merits of Og of Basan and Watersouchy of Amsterdam. Before a picture of Rubens or Murillo there was often a charming dissertation upon the pencil of Herr Sucrewasser of Vienna, or that great artist, Blunderbussiana of Venice. I used to listen unobserved until I was ready to kill myself with laughter, at the authorities quoted to the squires and farmers of Wiltshire, who took all for gospel. It was the most ridiculous thing in effect you can conceive. Between sixty and seventy years ago people did not know as much of the fine arts as they do now. Not but that they have still much to learn." The biographies of Aldrovandus Magnus of Bruges, of Andrew Guelph and Og of Basan, disciples of the former, of Sucrewasser of Vienna, Blunderbussiana of Dalmatia, and Watersouchy of Amsterdam, make up, as the author said in his last years, "a laughable book"; but, indeed, it is more than that, for it contains much brilliant satire on the Dutch and Flemish schools, showing that the writer, although so young, had profited by his early training in art. "[It is] a performance," Lockhart wrote in 1834, "in which the buoyancy of juvenile spirits sees of the results of already extensive observation, and the judgments of a refined (though far too fastidious and exclusive) taste."

In June 1780 Beckford, with Lettice again as his companion, went abroad for the second time, and visited Holland, Germany, Austria and Italy, staying for a while at Naples with his relative, Sir William Hamilton, whose first wife was then living. During this tour the young traveller made notes that soon after he expanded and printed under the title of "Dreams, Waking Thoughts, and Incidents." This book is composed of impressionist sketches made as his mind dictated, and nowhere did he allow himself to be shackled by the rules laid down by the compilers of works of travel. If anyone wants full particulars of a town, either topographical or historical, it is not to "Dreams, Waking Thoughts, and Incidents" he must turn; but if he desires exquisite word-pictures inspired by a brilliant imagination and conveyed with great literary skill, these he can find to his heart's content. The story goes that the book was suppressed by the author acting on the advice of his friends, who represented that the brilliant imagination therein displayed would create a prejudice against him when he should enter the practical field of public life, but it can scarcely be contended that this was the reason why at the eleventh hour it was withdrawn. As a matter of fact there were rumours, started no one knows how, of grave misconduct on Beckford's part, and probably it was thought that the tendency to romance laid bare in the work might give some colour to them. These rumours endured through Beckford's life, and the scandal was certainly widely circulated, but there seems to have been absolutely no grounds whatever for the charges. That Beckford should deny the charges was a matter of course, and, indeed, he protested passionately against them; but even John Mitford, an envenomed critic of his brother-author, had to admit that Samuel Richard White, Beckford's solicitor, who knew more about the matter than anyone else, after his client's death as during his life, declared his firm belief in Beckford's innocence.

In due course there were the coming-of-age festivities at Fonthill, and then another Continental tour, when Beckford was accompanied by so large a suite that at Augsburg he was mistaken for the Emperor of Austria, who at the time was known to be travelling incognito to Italy. Early in 1783, when he was two and twenty years of age, he came to England, saw, wooed, and married Lady Margaret Gordon, the sole surviving daughter of the Fourth Earl of Aboyne.

The years 1783 to 1786 make little call upon Beckford's biographer. The honeymoon had been spent in travelling, and when it was over the bride and bridegroom, still ardent lovers, stayed for a while at Cologny, near Geneva. Towards the end of the year, having made up their minds to sojourn for an indefinite period under southern skies, they decided to rent a more commodious residence, and took up their quarters at the Château de la Tour, near Vevey. There, in June 1784, was born a daughter, Susan Euphemia, and, on 14th May 1786, another, Margaret Maria Elizabeth. A fortnight later the young mother died. The marriage had been an ideal union, and Beckford's grief was terrible. His friends, fearful of his losing his reason or taking his life, moved him from place to place, hoping that change of scene might distract his thoughts, even momentarily, from the loss. To some extent this plan was successful, for after some weeks Beckford became again a reasonable being. He allowed arrangements to be made for his children to live with his mother, then residing at West End, between the villages of Hampstead and Kilburn; but himself continued to move restlessly from town to town, seeking, not change of place so much as change of thought. Though time mercifully mitigated the transports of his grief, it never ousted from his mind the memory of his gracious, beautiful wife. Rarely he spoke of her, but when he did mention her it was in a way which made it clear that she was always in his mind; though his wealth and genius made him the target of fortune-hunters, he never even thought to marry again; and his tender memories of her, enduring through the passage of years, acting upon an emotional nature, may have had more to do with his subsequent retirement than is generally supposed.

Before Beckford left England for his second Continental tour he had begun the composition of a "Suite des Contes arabes." Of this the principal story was "Vathek," which he completed while he was abroad. He sent the manuscript in 1783 to his friend, the Rev. Samuel Henley, who was delighted with it, and volunteered to translate it into English. The offer was accepted, but Henley proceeded leisurely with the work, which, with the notes added by him, was not finished until early in 1786. Beckford, however, was desirous to insert in "Vathek" the stories of the Princes whom his hero met in the Hall of Eblis, and he told Henley that on no account must the publication of the translation precede that of the original. Henley, however, ignored the author's injunction, and issued the translation later in the year, and made matters worse by stating that the tale was of Eastern origin: Beckford hereupon made the only rejoinder in his power, and issued the French original at Lausanne.

After bringing his children to England Beckford returned to the Continent, where he remained until 1794, visiting Spain and Portugal, where he wrote another book of travels, and staying for some time in Paris, where he witnessed the fall of the Bastille and the execution of Louis XVI. At Paris he was at one time mistaken for an English spy, and he was in danger of arrest, from which he was saved by the devotion of the second-hand bookseller, Chardin, who contrived his escape in disguise to England, for which he was rewarded by Beckford with a pension. Subsequently Beckford endeavoured, through his agent at Paris, to set on foot, in 1797, negotiations for a peace between France and this country.

After 1794 Beckford seldom left England except to pay brief visits to Paris. At Fonthill he employed James Wyatt, the architect, to make improvements in the house his father had built; and subsequently he erected a new house, the famous Fonthill Abbey, a magnificent but unsubstantial Gothic structure. Once Beckford was asked if the Abbey was built from his own plan. "No, I have sins enough to answer for, without having that laid to my charge," he answered. "Wyatt had an opportunity of raising a splendid monument to his fame, but he missed it." But whatever was said against the Abbey, no one had anything but praise for the gardens and park, which were, indeed, beautiful. Beckford lived at Fonthill until 1822, when, owing to the depreciation of his property in the West Indies, he sold the place and moved to Bath, where he remained until his death twenty-two years later.

Though Beckford had many visitors at Fonthill, he was singularly independent of company, having more resources in himself than usually falls to the lot of a man. "I love building, planting, gardening, whatever will keep me employed in the open air," he said; and, while the Abbey was being built and the grounds laid out, he might have been seen at all hours of the day, and sometimes, too, at night, watching the progress of the operations. He charged himself with the welfare of his workmen, of whom there were never less than two hundred in his employ; he visited the poor on his estates, and made provision for those who could not help themselves.

Beckford's indoor occupations were numerous. It has been said, and with some show of reason, that he was the most accomplished man of his time. He was a good musician, he could sketch, he spoke five modern European tongues, and could write three of them with elegance, he was well acquainted with Persian, Arabic, and, of course, the Latin and Greek classics; while his reading was at least as extensive as that of any of his contemporaries. Anyone who has these accomplishments can scarcely be dull, and Beckford, in addition, was an enthusiastic collector of books, pictures, and other treasures, in pursuit of which he frequently went to London to inspect the dealers' stocks of scarce volumes and fine paintings. Though he yielded to none in his love of tall copies, splendid bindings and rare editions, he was student as well as collector: and it was characteristic of his tastes that while, in later life, he sometimes disposed of a picture, he never sold a book. Even as in his youth he secluded himself at Lausanne to read Gibbon's library, which he had purchased, so afterwards he rarely put on his shelves any volume until he had made himself acquainted with its contents; and, large as his library was, to the end of his days he could without a moment's hesitation put his hand on any book or print he possessed. It was his habit to annotate his books, and to write some brief criticism on the fly-leaf. Sometimes his comments covered three or four pages, and one of the most valuable items offered at the sale of his library, in 1882–1883, was this item, knocked down to Quaritch for forty-two pounds: "Beckfordiana. Transcript from the autograph notes written by Mr Beckford on the fly-leaves of various works in his library, 7 vols., Manuscript (folio)." His comments were unusually shrewd, and often so caustic as to suggest that had he been obliged to earn his living he might well have turned an honest penny by contributing to one or other of the quarterlies in the days when severity was the motto of these periodicals.

In Wiltshire Beckford rarely went beyond the limits of his estate, except when driving to London; but at Bath he might occasionally be seen at a concert or a flower show, and not infrequently riding on his cream-coloured Arabian, either alone, attended by three grooms, two behind and one in front as an outrider, or in company with the Duke of Hamilton or a friend. He was always dressed in a great-coat with cloth buttons, a buff-striped waistcoat, breeches of the same kind of cloth as the coat, and brown top boots, the fine cotton stockings appearing over them, in the fashion of thirty or forty years before. He wore his hair powdered, and with his handsome face and fine eyes looked every inch the fine old English gentleman.

These appearances in public were the only difference between the life Beckford led at Fonthill and at Bath. In fine weather it was his invariable custom to rise early, ride to the tower he had erected at Lansdown, look at the flowers, and walk back to his house for breakfast. He would then read until noon, transact business with his steward, and afterwards ride out for exercise, again visiting the tower, if there was any planting or building going on. After dinner, which in those days was served in the afternoon, unless he had a visitor, he would retire to his library, and occupy himself with his correspondence, his books and his prints, and the examination of catalogues of sales sent to him by the London dealers. This routine was seldom varied, except when he went to London, where by this time he had removed from No. 22 Grosvenor Square to a house, No. 127 Park Street, overlooking Hyde Park, which, owing to its somewhat unwholesome insanitary condition, he styled, and dated from, "Cesspool House." In 1841, because of its many defects, he gave up this residence.

The Bath aristocracy and the fashionable folk who flocked to the watering-place could not understand how books and pictures, music and gardens, could occupy anyone to the exclusion of participation in the gaieties of the town; and the rumours that had been current in Wiltshire society were revived with interest in the little Somersetshire valley. The most awful crimes were placed to his account, and with them accusations of devil-worship and the study of astrology. Nothing was too terrible or too absurd with which to charge the man of mystery, and, we are told, "surmises were current about a brood of dwarfs that vegetated in an apartment built over the archway connecting his two houses; and the vulgar, rich and poor alike, gave a sort of half-credit to cabalistical monstrosities invoked in that apartment."

Though in his later years Beckford rarely indulged in the pleasures of authorship, he did not underrate his literary gifts, and he saw with pleasure that "Vathek" was taking the place in English literature to which it was entitled. New editions were called for, and in 1834 it took its place among Bentley's Standard Novels. The venture must have been profitable, for Bentley became Beckford's publisher-in-chief. He at once took over the "Biographical Memoirs of Extraordinary Painters," and in 1834 issued "Italy, with Sketches of Spain and Portugal"—a work that appeared in the same year also in Baudry's European Library, published in Paris. In 1835 Bentley brought out "Alcobaça and Batalha," and five years later republished this and the earlier book of travels in one volume—the last edition of any of Beckford's books issued in the author's lifetime. Beckford's interest in the various publications was very considerable, and his annoyance with adverse critics is only to be compared with the anger he displayed when rival collectors at auction sales snatched treasures from his grasp. The adverse critics of "Italy, with Sketches of Spain and Portugal," however, were few and far between. It was, indeed, received with a chorus of praise, and no one cried "Bravo!" louder than Lockhart, who reviewed the work in *The Quarterly Review*.

Though Beckford lived to the patriarchal age of eighty-four, almost to the last hour of his life he enjoyed good health. It has already been said that when nearly eighty he declared he had never known a moment's *ennui*: few men have been able to say so much; yet there is no doubt this was true, for he had stumbled upon the secret that only the idle man is bored. Beckford was never idle; he had made so many interests for himself that every moment of his day was occupied. A man of his age who, in his last weeks, retains all his enthusiasms for his books, his prints and his gardens, may well claim that he has made a success of life. His intellectual power never waned, his sight was preserved to him unimpaired, and at seventy-eight he could read from manuscript for an hour and a half without resting. When his last illness overtook him, he was busily engaged in marking a catalogue of M. Nodier's library, the sale of which at Paris his agent was to attend to make purchases: he was as enthusiastic about his collections at the age of eighty-four as he had been when he took up his residence at Fonthill fifty years before.

Physically, too, considering his great age, he was wonderfully active, and until within a few days of his death he took regular exercise on foot and on horseback. When he was seventy-seven he astonished a friend by mentioning that he had on the previous day at dusk ridden from Cheapside to his house in Park Street; and a year later he stated, "I never feel fatigue. I can walk twenty to thirty miles a day; and I only use my carriage (in London) on account of its being convenient to put a picture or book into it, which I happen to purchase in my rambles." At seventy-five his activity was so great that he could mount rapidly to the top of the tower at Lansdown without halting—"no small exertion," comments Cyrus Redding feelingly, "for many who were fifteen or twenty years younger": and even eight years later, during his visits to London, he would ride to Hampstead Heath, or through Hyde Park, and along the Edgware Road to West End, and pull up his horse opposite the spot where once had been the entrance to his mother's house.

Most men who live to an advanced age have some theory to account for it. Beckford had none, beyond believing that his days had probably been prolonged by the fact that his life had been temperate, and that, as he grew older, he took reasonable care of himself. "I enjoy too good health, feel too happy, and am too much pleased with life to have any inclination to throw it away for want of attention," he said. "When I am summoned I must go, though I should not much mind living another hundred years, and, as far as my health goes at present, I see no reason why I should not." Thus, when going out he would put on an overcoat, even if there were only the slightest wind stirring; and, however interested or amused he might be, he would always retire early; but while he took such precautions as these, he was in no sense a valetudinarian. His love of fresh air, and his activity, together with the regular life he led, undoubtedly had much to do with his attaining his great age.

Until the last week of April 1844, Beckford occupied himself in his usual way, walking and riding, and working in his library. Then influenza laid hold of him, and though he struggled manfully against it, at last there was no doubt that the end was near. He sent a last laconic note to his surviving daughter, the Duchess of Hamilton, "Come quick! quick!" and a day or two after her arrival, on 2nd May, he expired, with perfect resignation, and, we are told, so peacefully that those by his side could not tell the moment when he passed away.

His mortal remains were, on 11th May, interred in the Bath Abbey Cemetery; but soon after they were removed, and reburied, more appropriately, at Lansdown, under the shadow of his tower. On one side of his tomb is a quotation from "Vathek," "Enjoying humbly the most precious gift of heaven to man—Hope"; and on another these lines from his poem, "A Prayer":

"Eternal Power!

Grant me, through obvious clouds one transient gleam

Of thy bright essence in my dying hour."

Charles James Fox

Charles James Fox, one of the most brilliant personalities, if not, indeed, the most brilliant personality, that flourished in the last decades of the eighteenth century, was the third son of Henry Fox, afterwards Baron Holland of Foxley, and Lady Georgiana Lennox, daughter of Charles, second Duke of Richmond, a grandson of Charles II. The future statesman was born on 24th January 1749, and as he grew up it was thought that a resemblance to his royal ancestor could be traced in his dark, harsh and saturnine features, that "derived a sort of majesty from the addition of two black and shaggy eyebrows, which sometimes concealed, but more frequently developed, the workings of his mind." He was a bright, lively and original child, but subject to violent excesses of temper. "Charles is dreadfully passionate," said his mother. "What shall we do with him?" "Oh, never mind. He is a very sensible little fellow, and he will learn to cure himself," replied his father, who perceived and was proud of the lad's unusual ability. "Let nothing be done to break his spirit; the world will effect that business soon enough."

At a private school at Wandsworth, and subsequently at Eton, where Dr Philip Francis was his private tutor, the lad showed himself both intelligent and diligent. His education was interrupted in 1763, when his father took him to Paris and Spa, and at that early age initiated him into the mysteries of gaming, the passion for which was subsequently to exercise a most adverse influence on him. On his return to Eton his newly acquired knowledge of the world demoralised his companions, and he gave himself airs and thought himself a man until the headmaster birched him, and so brought him down to earth. In 1764 he went to Hertford College, Oxford, preceded by a reputation for Latin verse, a considerable knowledge of French, and a power of oratory unusual in one so young, but which he attributed to the fact that at home he had always been encouraged to think freely, and as freely to express his opinions. At the University he read deeply in classics and history, and the taste then developed endured through life, for, while he indulged in many frivolities, he would in the midst of them steal a few hours to devote to the books of which he never wearied. Towards the end of his days he put his learning into harness, and wrote a history of the reign of James II. and an account of the Revolution of 1688 that do not deserve to be relegated to obscurity.

Much has been written about the faults of Fox, but some of them, at least, should not be held greatly to his discredit, since they were the faults of the age. Wine, women and cards were the occupations of his companions, and not of the unintelligent only. Everybody drank and drank deeply, drank in pursuit of pleasure, drank to drown sorrow.

"I dined at Holland House" (wrote the Right Honourable Charles Rigby upon one occasion to George Selwyn), "where, though I drank claret with the master of it from dinner till two in the morning, I could not wash away the sorrow he is in at the shocking condition his eldest boy is in."

Fox, Sheridan, Pitt and, notably, Professor Porson were three-bottle men, and it was not unusual for politicians to go to Westminster Hall in a state of insobriety.

"Fox drinks what I should call a great deal, though he is not reckoned to do so by his companions; Sheridan, excessively, and Grey more than any of them; while Pitt, I am told, drinks as much as anybody, generally more than any of his company, and is a pleasant, convivial man at table,"

Sir Gilbert Elliot has recorded; and Lord Bulkeley wrote to the Marquis of Buckingham à propos of Pitt bringing in the Declaratory Bill of the powers of the Board of Control:

"It was an awkward day for him (owing to the defection of some friends), and he felt it the more because he himself was low-spirited, and overcome by the heat of the House, in consequence of having got drunk the night before at your house in Pall Mall, with Mr Dundas and the *Duchess of Gordon*! They must have had a hard bout of it, for even Dundas, who is well used to the bottle, was affected by it, and spoke remarkably ill, dull and tedious."

One reads with amazement of a Chancellor of the Exchequer, a Lord Chancellor and a Treasurer of the Navy—Pitt, Thurlow and Dundas— excited by wine galloping through a turnpike gate without paying the toll, and the man, mistaking them for highwaymen, discharging his blunderbuss. This exploit was duly noted in "The Rolliad."

"Ah! think what danger on debauch attends!

Let Pitt o'er wine preach temperance to his friends,

How, as he wandered darkling o'er the plain,

His reason drowned in Jenkinson's champagne,

A rustic's hand, but righteous fate withstood,

Had shed a Premier's for a robber's blood."

A great drinker, too, was Jack Talbot of the Coldstream Guards, and it was of him, when the doctor said: "My lord, he is in a bad way, for I was obliged to make use of the lancet this morning," that the witty Alvanley remarked: "You should have *tapped* him, Doctor, for I am sure he has more claret than blood in his veins." Another was the eccentric Twistleton Fiennes, Lord Saye and Sele, a famous epicure, who drank large quantities of absinthe and curaçoa. Gronow recommended him a servant, who, arriving as Fiennes was going to dinner, asked his new master if he had any orders, only to receive these instructions: "Place two bottles of sherry by my bedside, and call me the day after to-morrow!"

Gambling vied with drinking as an amusement of the aristocracy, and the one was as ruinous to their purses as the other to their health. Everyone played cards in those days, and even ladies gambled with as much zest as their husbands and brothers. There was much card-playing in private houses, but more in the clubs, especially at White's, Brooks's and Almack's.

"As the gambling and extravagance of the young men of fashion has arrived now at a pitch never heard of, it is worth while to give some account of it" (Walpole wrote in 1772). "They have a club at Almack's in Pall Mall, where they played only for rouleaus of fifty pounds each rouleau; and generally there was ten thousand pounds in specie on the table. Lord Holland had paid about twenty thousand pounds for his two sons. Nor were the manners of the gamesters, or even their dresses for play, undeserving notice. They began by pulling off their embroidered clothes, and put on frieze great-coats, or turned their coats inside outwards for luck. They put on pieces of leather (such as is worn by footmen when they clean knives) to save their lace ruffles; and to guard their eyes from the light and prevent tumbling their hair, wore high-crowned straw hats with broad brims, and adorned with flowers and ribbons; masks to conceal their emotions when they played at quinze. Each gamester had a small, neat stand by him, with a large rim, to hold their tea, or a wooden bowl with an edge of ormolu to hold their rouleaus. They borrowed great sums of the Jews at exorbitant premiums. Charles Fox called his outward room, where those Jews waited till he rose, the Jerusalem Chamber. His brother Stephen was enormously fat; George Selwyn said he was in the right to deal with Shylocks, as he could give them 'pounds of flesh.' "

Charles James Fox

It is not exaggeration to say that during the long sittings at macao, hazard, and faro many tens of thousands exchanged hands.

Fox was a magnificent player of piquet and whist, but in the evenings, when he had dined well and wined well, he would play only games of chance, at which he was always unlucky.

"At Almack's of pigeons I'm told there are flocks,

But it's thought the completest is one Mr Fox.

If he touches a card, if he rattles a box,

Away fly the guineas of this Mr Fox."

Once, before delivering a speech in defence of the Church, he played for twenty-two hours, and lost five hundred pounds an hour; and then declared that the greatest pleasure in life, after winning, was losing! His bad luck was notorious, but again and again his intimates came to his assistance, and Walpole wondered what he would do when he had sold the estates of all his friends! It was noticed that he did not do himself justice in a debate on the Thirty-Nine Articles (6th February 1772), and Walpole thought it was not to be wondered at.

"He had sat up playing at hazard at Almack's from Tuesday evening, the 4th, till five in the afternoon of Wednesday, 5th. An hour before, he had recovered twelve thousand pounds that he had lost, and by dinner, which was at five o'clock, he had ended losing eleven thousand pounds. On the Thursday he spoke in the above debate, went to dinner at half-past eleven at night, from there to White's, where he drank till seven the next morning, thence to Almack's, where he won six thousand pounds, and between three and four in the afternoon he set out for Newmarket. His brother Stephen lost ten thousand pounds two nights after, and Charles eleven thousand pounds more on the 13th, so that in three nights the two brothers, the eldest not twenty-four, lost thirty-two thousand pounds."

The wonder is, not that Fox spoke ill, but that he spoke at all.

They were good losers in those days, and stoicism was a very necessary quality to be possessed by the majority, since all played and few won. One night, when Fox had been terribly unfortunate at the faro-table, Topham Beauclerk followed him to his rooms to offer consolation, expecting to find him perhaps stretched on the floor bewailing his losses, perhaps plunged in moody despair. He was surprised to see him reading Herodotus. "What would you have me do?" Fox asked the astonished visitor. "I have lost my last shilling." "Charles tells me he has not now, nor has had for some time, one guinea," Lord Carlisle told George Selwyn, "and is happier on that account."

"But hark! the voice of battle shouts from far,

The Jews and Macaronis are at war;

The Jews prevail, and, thund'ring from the stocks,

They seize, they bind, they circumcise Charles Fox."

The money-lenders were most obliging to Fox at the time when he was heir-apparent to the barony of Holland, but the holder of the title had an heir, which destroyed his prospects; whereupon Fox, unperturbed, made it the subject of a joke against his creditors: "My brother Ste's son is a second Messiah, born for the destruction of the Jews." He lived on credit for some time, and so notorious was this fact that when he gave a supper-party at his rooms in St James's Street, close by Brooks's Club, Tickell addressed verses thereon to Sheridan:

"Derby shall send, if not his plate, his cooks;

And know, I've bought the best champagne from Brooks,

From liberal Brooks, whose speculative skill

Is hasty credit and a distant bill;

Who, nursed on clubs, disdains a vulgar trade,

Exults to trust, and blushes to be paid."

Lord Holland had already paid his son's debts on several occasions, and apparently some remonstrance was addressed to the latter.

"In regard to what you say of my father's feelings, I am sure if you could have known how very miserable you have made me you would not have said it" (Fox wrote in 1773 to Lady Holland, in a letter in which there is the true note of sincerity). "To be loved by you and him has always been (indeed, I am no hypocrite, whatever I may be) the first desire of my life. The reflection that I have behaved ill to you is almost the only painful one I have ever experienced. That my extreme imprudence and dissipation has given both of you uneasiness is what I have long known, and I am sure I may call those who really know me to witness how much that thought has embittered my life. I own I lately began to flatter myself that, particularly with you, and in a great measure with my father, I had regained that sort of confidence which was once the greatest pride of my life; and I am sure I don't exaggerate when I say that, since I formed those flattering hopes, I have been the happiest being in the universe. I hate to make professions, and yet I think I may venture to say that my conduct in the future shall be such as to satisfy you more than my past. Indeed, indeed, my dear mother, no son ever loved a father and mother as I do. Pray, my dear mother, consider how very miserable you have made me, and pity me. I do not know what to write, so have to leave off writing, but you may be assured that no son ever felt more duty, respect, gratitude, or love than I do for both of you, and that it is in your power, by restoring me to your usual confidence and affection, or depriving me of it, to make me the most unhappy or contented of men."

Once again Lord Holland took upon himself the settlement of Charles's debt, and just before his death, in 1774, satisfied his son's creditors—at a cost of £140,000! Even this was not a sufficient lesson to the young man, who incurred fresh liabilities, to pay which he sold a sinecure place of £2000 a year for life—the Clerkship of the Peels in Ireland, and the superbly decorated mansion and estate at Kingsgate in the Isle of Thanet, both of which had been left him by his father.

Fox in his twentieth year entered Parliament as member for the pocket borough of Midhurst in Sussex, and, at his father's request, supported the Duke of Grafton's administration. He took his seat in May 1768, and distinguished himself in the following year by a speech opposing the claim of Wilkes to take his seat as member for Middlesex. "It was all off-hand, all argumentative, in reply to Mr Burke and Mr Wedderburn, and excessively well indeed," Lord Holland said proudly. "I hear it spoken of as an extraordinary thing, and I am, as you see, not a little pleased with it." This was the age of young men, for Fox's lifelong antagonist, Pitt, entered the House when he was twenty-two, accepted the Chancellorship of the Exchequer twelve months later, and became Prime Minister in his twenty-fifth year! The careers of these statesmen must have delighted another precocious genius, Benjamin Disraeli, who reverenced youth. "The only tolerable thing in life is action, and action is feeble without youth," he wrote. "What if you do not obtain your immediate object? You always think you will, and the detail of the adventure is full of rapture." The blunders of youth, that great man thought, are preferable to the triumph of manhood or the successes of old age.

In February 1770 Fox took office under Lord North as Lord of the Admiralty, when, owing to his attitude in the debates on the Press laws, he became so unpopular with a section of the public as actually to be attacked in the streets, and rolled in the mud. It has already been mentioned how, in February 1772, he spoke against the clerical petition for relief from subscription to the Thirty-Nine Articles; and later, in the same month, he resigned his office so as to be free to oppose the Royal Marriage Bill, which was introduced by the King's command after the announcement of the Duke of Cumberland's marriage with Mrs Horton. The King was determined, so far as it lay in his power, to prevent the occurrence in his family of another *mésalliance*, and the principal clauses of the Royal Marriage Act forbade the marriage of a member of the royal family under the age of twenty-five without the consent of the monarch, and above that age, if the King refused consent, without the permission of both Houses of Parliament. The Bill was fiercely contested in both Houses of Parliament; Fox, Burke, and Wedderburn were its most strenuous opponents in the Commons; Lord Folkestone, in person, and Lord Chatham, by letter, in the Lords. It was denounced by its opponents as "un-English, arbitrary, and contrary to the law of God"; and the objection raised was that it would set the royal family as a caste apart. So unpopular was it that, in spite of the King's influence being exerted in its favour, an amendment limiting it to the reign of George III. and three years longer was negatived only by a majority of eighteen. The Bill became law in March 1772.

Fox began to be recognised as a power in the House, and Lord North soon made overtures to his erstwhile colleague to rejoin the ministry as a Lord of the Treasury. This Fox did within a year of his resignation, but his independence soon brought about another rupture; and when, on a question of procedure, he caused the defeat of the ministry by pressing a motion to a division, the King wrote to Lord North: "Indeed, that young man has so thoroughly cast off every principle of common honour and honesty that he must become as contemptible as he is odious, and I hope you will let him know you are not insensible of his conduct towards you." The Prime Minister took the hint, and dismissed Fox in a delightfully laconic note: "Sir, His Majesty has thought proper to order a new Commission of the Treasury, in which I do not see your name."

In opposition Fox was a vigorous opponent of Lord North's policy in connection with the American colonies. In April 1774 he voted for the repeal of the tea duty, declaring that the tax was the mere assertion of a right that would force the colonists into open rebellion; and he attacked the subsequent proceedings of the English government on account of their manifest injustice. Against the war that ensued he protested with might and main, and to the utmost of his power tried to force the ministry into a pacific path.

"The war of the Americans is a war of passion" (he declared on 26th November 1778); "it is of such a nature as to be supported by the most powerful virtues, love of liberty and of country, and at the same time by those passions in the human heart which give courage, strength and perseverance to man; the spirit of revenge for the injury you have done them, of retaliation for the hardships inflicted on them, and of opposition to the unjust powers you would have exercised over them; everything combines to animate them to this war, and such a war is without end; for whatever obstinacy enthusiasm ever inspired man with, you will now have to contend with in America; no matter what gives birth to that enthusiasm, whether the name of religion or of liberty, the effects are the same; it inspires a spirit that is unconquerable and solicitous to undergo difficulties and dangers; and as long as there is a man in America, so long will you have him against you in the field."

And in the following year he compared George III. with Henry VI.—"both owed the Crown to revolutions, both were pious princes, and both lost the acquisitions of their predecessors"—and so earned the enmity of the King, who could not differentiate between doctrine and action; and because Fox supported the rights of the Americans looked upon him henceforth as a rebel. Later, when of all the colonies only Boston remained in the hands of the English, and Wedderburn with foolhardy audacity ventured in the House of Commons to compare North as a War Minister with Chatham, Fox created a sensation by declaring that "not Lord Chatham, nor Alexander the Great, nor Cæsar ever conquered so much territory in the course of all their wars as Lord North had lost in one campaign!" In January 1781 he made a further effort, in which he was supported by Pitt, to compel Lord North to abandon the war and make peace with the colonies.

"The only objection made to my motion" (he declared) "is that it must lead to American independence. But I venture to assert that *within six months of the present day*, Ministers themselves will come forward to Parliament with some proposition of a similar nature. I know that such is their intention; I announce it to the House."

Of course his resolution was defeated, and the colonies were for ever lost to the Crown. "I that am born a gentleman," said George III. to Lord Thurlow and the Duke of Leeds, "shall never lay my head on my last pillow in peace and quiet as long as I remember the loss of my American colonies." Not the less, the King never forgave Fox for that attitude which might have averted the disaster.

Fox, who had declined office in 1780, was two years later appointed Foreign Secretary when Lord Rockingham became Prime Minister, and in this position he won golden opinions.

"Mr Fox already shines as greatly in place as he did in opposition, though infinitely more difficult a task" (Walpole wrote to Mr Horace Mann). "He is now as indefatigable as he was idle. He has perfect temper, and not only good humour and good nature, but, which is the first quality of a Prime Minister in a free country, has more common sense than any man, with amazing parts that are neither ostentatious nor affected."

Lord Rockingham died a few months later, when Lord Shelburne was appointed in his place, and soon after Fox, with some of his colleagues, withdrew from the Ministry. The cause of his secession was said to be that Fox wished to grant independence to the American colonies as a boon, and Lord Shelburne would regard it only as a bargain; but the underlying reasons were Fox's hatred of the man and jealousy aroused by the exclusion from office of the Duke of Portland. It was to Lord Shelburne, who was most unpopular and suspected of insincerity, that Goldsmith made his singularly *mal à propos* remark: "Do you know, I could never conceive the reason why they call you Malagrida, for Malagrida was a very good sort of man!"

Fox allied himself with Lord North, and as they had a large majority in the House of Commons, Lord Shelburne resigned in February 1784. The King was furious, but being powerless, was compelled to appoint as First Minister of the Crown the Duke of Portland, under whom Pitt and Lord North held office as Secretaries of State.

In the previous year the Prince of Wales had come of age, and had at once attached himself to the Opposition, who naturally welcomed so powerful an ally.

"The Prince of Wales has thrown himself into the arms of Charles, and this in the most indecent and undisguised manner" (Walpole wrote to Sir Horace Mann). "Fox lodged in St James's Street, and as soon as he rose, which was very late, held a *levée* of his followers, and of the members of the Gambling Club at Brooks's, all his disciples. His bristly, black person, and shagged breast quite open, and rarely purified by any ablutions, was wrapped in a foul linen night-gown, and his bushy hair dishevelled. In these cynic weeds, and with epicurean good humour, did he dictate his politics, and in this school did the heir to the Crown attend his lessons and imbibe them."

Fox told his new adherent that a Prince of Wales should have no party, but, his advice being disregarded, when the opinion was expressed that the Prince should not attend the debates in the House of Commons, he intervened in defence of his friend.

"Is the mind, which may at any hour, by the common changes of mortality, be summoned to the highest duties allotted to man, to be left to learn them by accident?" (he asked). "For my part I rejoice to see this distinguished person disdaining to use the privileges of his rank and keep aloof from the debates of this House. I rejoice to see him manfully coming among us, to imbibe a knowledge of the Constitution within the walls of the Commons of England. I, for my part, see nothing in the circumstance which has called down so much voluntary eloquence."

There were many, however, who disapproved of this alliance, and many attacks were made upon Fox, who was the subject of many lampoons.

"Though matters at present go cross in the realm,

You will one day be K——g, Sir, and I at the helm;

So let us be jovial, drink, gamble and sing,

Nor regard it a straw, tho' we're not yet the thing.

Tol de rol, tol, tol, tol de rol."

The principal act of the Administration was the introduction of Fox's India Bill, by which powers were sought to take away the control of the great dominion that Warren Hastings had built up from the Honourable East India Company and transfer it to a board of seven Commissioners, who should hold office for five years and be removable only on an Address to the Crown from either House of Parliament. This was bitterly opposed by the merchant class, who saw in it a precedent for the revocation of other charters; but the clause that aroused the greatest bitterness was that in which it was laid down that the appointment of the first seven Commissioners should be vested in Parliament, and afterwards in the Crown. This was, of course, equivalent to vesting the appointments and the enormous patronage attaching thereto in the Ministry, and "it was an attempt," said Lord Thurlow, "to take the diadem from the King's head and to put it on that of Mr Fox." The Bill was fought with every weapon, but it passed the Commons, only, however, to be defeated by the Lords, upon whom the King had brought his personal influence to bear. Thereupon, in December 1783, the King contemptuously dismissed the Ministry.

In the following May there was a General Election, the chief interest of which centred round the City of Westminster, for which Fox and Sir Cecil Wray had sat in the dissolved Parliament. The King, who had plotted the downfall of the Ministry, had determined to do his utmost to prevent Fox from sitting in the new Parliament, but the latter, who had, however, already been elected for Kirkwall, audaciously carried the war into the enemy's camp by having himself nominated for his old constituency.

"It may fairly be questioned" (Mr Sidney said) "whether any of the electoral contests of the eighteenth century equalled that of Westminster in point of the prevalence of corrupt practices, drunkenness, tumult and disorder. The polling lasted forty days, and, during the long period over which it extended, the entire western quarter of the Metropolis and Covent Garden, the immediate vicinity of the hustings, presented a scene of uproar and disorder which it is difficult to describe. The latter locality might have been styled 'Bear Garden' for the time being, so flagrant were the outrages against decency, and so riotous was the violence of which it was the scene."

At first the two Ministerial candidates, Admiral Hood and Sir Cecil Wray, forged ahead, and left Fox so far behind that the prospect of his return appeared hopeless. Then the influence of the many ladies of rank and fashion who canvassed for the latter made itself felt. The Duchess of Portland, Countess Carlisle, Countess of Derby, Lady Beauchamp, and Lady Duncannon were among Fox's assistants, but the greatest service was rendered by the beautiful Duchess of Devonshire, whose charms have been chronicled by every contemporary memorist.

"Array'd in matchless beauty, Devon's fair

In Fox's favour takes a zealous part;

But oh! where'er the pilferer comes, beware:

She supplicates a vote, and steals a heart!"

A reaction in favour of Fox set in, and when, at three o'clock on 17th May, the poll closed, the High Bailiff of Westminster declared the results:

"Lord Hood	6694
Hon. C. J. Fox	6234
Sir Cecil Wray	5998
	————
Majority for Fox	236"

Great were the rejoicings when it became known that "the man of the people" had snatched the victory from the Court candidate. The Prince of Wales, who had thrown his influence into the scale, went the same evening to a supper-party given by Mrs Crewe, where all present were arrayed in buff and blue, the victor's colours. The Prince proposed the health of the hostess with felicitous brevity, "True Blue and Mrs Crewe," to which the lady wittily replied, "True Blue, and all of you"; and the hero of the hour returned thanks to all and sundry.

It was to Mr Fox and Mrs Armitstead (with whom Fox was then living and whom he married in 1795), at the latter's house at St Anne's, Chertsey, that the Prince repaired to pour out his woes when, to evade his compromising attentions, Mrs Fitzherbert went abroad.

"Mrs Armitstead has repeatedly assured me" (Lord Holland relates in his "Memoirs of the Whig Party") "that he came thither more than once to converse with her and Mr Fox on the subject, that he cried by the hour, that he testified to the sincerity and violence of his passion and his despair by the most extravagant expressions and actions, rolling on the floor, striking his forehead, tearing his hair, falling into hysterics, and swearing he would abandon the country, forego the Crown, sell his jewels and plate, and scrape together a competence to fly with the object of his affections to America."

When Mrs Fitzherbert returned to England, Fox implored the Prince not to marry her, and received from him a reply, "Make yourself easy, my dear friend! Believe me, the world will soon be convinced that not only is there not, but never was, any grounds for these reports, which have been so malevolently circulated." On the strength of this letter, when the question was raised in the House of Commons in a debate on the Prince's debts, Fox denied the marriage, only to be told by a relative of the lady at Brooks's Club, within an hour of his speech, that the marriage had taken place! It is said that the statesman was furious at the deception that had been practised upon him; but doubtless his sense of humour came to his rescue: one can imagine him shrugging his shoulders with his almost imperturbable good humour, as he reflected that while his position as a dupe was distressing, what must be the feeling of him who had duped him. It was, indeed, a case of the biter bit! Perhaps, too, he was amused at having saved the Prince *malgré lui*; and certainly it is to his credit that "when urged by his friends to undeceive Parliament, and thus vindicate himself in the opinion of the country, he refused to do so at the expense of the heir to the monarchy." But there was on his part a coldness towards the Prince for some time, and he never again trusted that royal personage.

It is impossible within the limits of this paper to discuss Fox's subsequent political career, or to make more than an allusion to the attacks on Warren Hastings during the famous impeachment, to his advocacy of the Prince as the rightful Regent during the King's illness, and his opposition to many of Pitt's measures. His remark on hearing of the taking of the Bastille has become historic: "How much is this the greatest event that ever happened in the world, and how much the best"; but he never approved of the excesses that followed, and he was opposed to all absolute forms of government, and not more averse to an absolute monarchy or an absolute aristocracy than to an absolute democracy. From 1792 for five years he seldom attended Parliament, but devoted himself chiefly to the composition of his "History of the Revolution of 1688." In 1798 his name was erased from the list of Privy Councillors because at a dinner he proposed the toast of "Our Sovereign, the people." Later he went abroad, had an interview with Napoleon, and on his return, in 1803, in a magnificent speech advocated a peace with France. On Lord Addington's resignation in the following year it was proposed that Fox should be a member of the new Cabinet, but the King intervened to make Pitt promise, firstly, never to support Catholic Emancipation, and, secondly, to exclude Fox from office. However, two years later, Fox accepted the portfolio of the Foreign Office under Grenville, in the "Ministry of all the Talents." He made his last appearance in the House of Commons on 10th June 1806, to move a resolution preparatory to introducing a Bill for the suppression of the slave trade.

"So fully am I impressed with the vast importance and necessity of attaining what will be the object of my motion this night" (he concluded his farewell speech) "that if, during the almost forty years that I have had the honour of a seat in Parliament, I had been so fortunate as to accomplish that, and that only, I should think I had done enough, and could retire from public life with comfort and the conscious satisfaction that I had done my duty."

A few days after, he was taken ill at the house of the Duke of Devonshire at Chiswick, and it was soon apparent that his last hours were near. He was no believer in religion, but, to please his wife, he consented to have prayers read, though he "paid little attention to the ceremony, remaining quiescent merely, not liking to refuse any wish of hers, nor to pretend any sentiments he did not entertain." "I die happy," he said to his wife, "but I pity you." He died on 13th September, and was interred in Westminster Abbey, immediately adjoining the monument of Lord Chatham, and close by the grave of William Pitt, his great rival, who had predeceased him by a few months.

As a constructive statesman, Charles James Fox had but little opportunity to shine.

"Charles is unquestionably a man of first rate talents, but so deficient in judgment as never to have succeeded in any object during his whole life" (said his "candid friend," Boothby). "He loved only three things, women, play, and politics. Yet at no period did he ever form a creditable connection with a woman. He lost his whole fortune at the gaming table; and, with the exception of about eleven months of his life, he has remained always in opposition."

This is a severe pronouncement upon a great man, who was a great orator and a splendid debater.

"Fox delivered his speeches without previous preparation, and their power lay not in rhetorical adornments, but in the vigour of the speaker's thoughts, the extent of his knowledge, the quickness with which he grasped the significance of each point in debate, the clearness of his conceptions, and the remarkable plainness with which he laid them before his audience" (says Professor Harrison). "Even in the longest speeches he never strayed from the matter in hand; he never rose above the level of his hearers' understanding, was never obscure, and never bored the House. Every position that he took up he defended by a large number of shrewd arguments, plainly stated and well ordered."

His voice was poor, his actions ungainly, and he did not become fluent until he warmed with his subject; but in attack generally, and especially in connection with the American War, Grattan thought him the best speaker he had ever heard. Burke said he was "the most brilliant and accomplished debater that the world ever saw"; Rogers declared he "never heard anything equal to Fox's *speeches in reply*"; while, when someone abused one of Fox's speeches to Pitt, the latter remarked, "Don't disparage it; nobody could have made it but himself."

Fox, however, did not lay undue stress on eloquence, and in a well-known speech declared that one sometimes paid too dearly for oratory.

"I remember" (he said) "a time when the whole of the Privy Council came away, throwing up their caps, and exulting in an extraordinary manner at a speech made by the present Lord Rosslyn (Alexander Wedderburn), and an examination of Dr Franklin (before the Privy Council on the letters of Hutchinson and Oliver, the Governor and Lieutenant-Governor of Massachusetts), in which that respectable man was most uncommonly badgered. But we paid very dear for that splendid specimen of eloquence, and all its attendant tropes, figures, metaphors, and hyperbole; for then came the Bill, and in the end we lost all our American colonies, a hundred millions of money, and a hundred thousand of our brave fellow subjects."

Fox made mistakes occasionally, as when he asserted the *right* of the Prince of Wales to the Regency; but he was distinguished in the House of Commons for his "hopeful sympathy with all good and great causes." In a day when politicians were not especially enlightened, he was a supporter of Parliamentary reform, a champion of Catholic Emancipation, and an opponent of the slave trade; and, indeed, it was by his advocacy of these measures that he earned the enmity of the King, and thus was prevented from carrying out these beneficial schemes.

It has already been admitted that he was a spendthrift, and had a passion for gaming which, when taxed with it by Lord Hillsborough in the House of Commons, he designated as "a vice countenanced by the fashion of the times, a vice to which some of the greatest characters had given way in the early part of their lives, and a vice which carried with it its own punishment." His weaknesses, however, were more than balanced by his many splendid qualities. He was a noble antagonist, and when Pitt made his first speech, and someone remarked he would be one of the first in Parliament, "He is so already," said Fox. Which recalls the story of the Prince of Wales' remark, on hearing of the death of the Duchess of Devonshire: "Then we have lost the best-bred woman in England." "Then," said the more generous Fox, "we have lost the kindest heart in England."

Fox was a great-hearted man, with a beautiful disposition, high spirits, unbounded good-humour, delightful conversation, a great affection for his friends, an undeniable loyalty to those who trusted him; and these qualities, combined with his great natural abilities and an indisputable charm, made him a great, commanding and fascinating figure. Gibbon, a political opponent, said he possessed "the powers of a superior man, as they are blended in his attractive character, with the softness and simplicity of a child," adding that "perhaps no human being was ever more perfectly exempt from the taint of malevolence, vanity or falsehood"; but the greatest tribute came from Burke, who described him simply and, perhaps, sufficiently as "a man made to be loved."

Philip, Duke of Wharton

In the history of every country a few figures stand out conspicuous, not necessarily for ability or virtue, or even vice, but through the power of a dominating personality or the strangeness of their career. In the Georgian annals of England in the forefront of these heroes of romance stands, head and shoulders above the rest, Charles James Fox, whose genius and fascinations, indeed, whose very faults, seize the imagination, and hold it captive, a willing prisoner; but there are others, minor lights to this great star, yet still shining so brightly as to dazzle the sober senses of twentieth-century social historians, a body not given unduly to hero-worship. Such a one was Brummell, another was "Beau" Nash, both arbiters of fashion, veritable kings in the eyes of their contemporaries; a third was Elizabeth Chudleigh, Countess of Bristol, Duchess of Kingston, greater still as Beatrix, queen of hearts, in "Esmond"; and to a place in this gallery of adventurous spirits none can deny the right of Philip, Duke of Wharton, Richardson's Lovelace, gallant, wit, statesman, satirist, poet and pamphleteer, like Dryden's Zimri, "everything by starts and nothing long," a man who threw away great gifts, honour, loyalty and love, as freely, and with as little regard for consequences, as Fox squandered his gold.

Philip, born on Christmas Eve, 1698, was the only son of Thomas, fourth Baron Wharton, by his second wife, Lucy, daughter of Lord Lisburne, who in that year was a toast at the Kit-Cat Club:

"When Jove to Ida did the gods invite,

And in immortal toastings pass'd the night,

With more than bowls of nectar were they blest,

For Venus was the Wharton of the feast!"

Lord Wharton—for his services to William III. created in 1706 earl, when his heir became known as Viscount Winchendon—was not only a pleasure-loving man, but also a strenuous politician. He, imbued with the idea that his boy, in his turn, might add further laurels to the family name, with this object in view kept a more than paternal eye upon the direction of the youngster's studies. To his parents' great joy, Philip gave signs of precocious cleverness, and it was decided to have him educated by private tutors, instructed, after their pupil was well grounded in the classics, to teach him in a very thorough manner the history of Europe, with, of course, special reference to that of his own country; and to train him as an orator by making him read and recite passages from Shakespeare and from the great speeches of the most eloquent statesmen of that and bygone ages.

Philip evinced much readiness, and diligently applied himself to his studies; but his father's love of pleasure was in his blood, and while for some time he submitted to the company of his teachers, with little or no relaxation from his books, at last, as was only to be expected from a high-spirited lad, he broke over the traces. Handsome and graceful, he found his pleasure with women: a fault which his father, now created Marquis of Wharton, could overlook in consideration of his son's promise in other directions. However, the young man destroyed all the Marquis's hope of an alliance with some lady of high rank and vast wealth by secretly espousing, at the Fleet, on 2nd March 1715, when he was in his seventeenth year, Martha, the penniless daughter of Major-General Holmes—a proceeding that the Marquis took so much to heart that, it was said, his death six weeks later was directly attributable to his grief and anger.

The effects of this madcap escapade might not have been very serious, for there was nothing to be urged against the girl except her lack of money and great connections, if the accomplished fact had been recognised in the right spirit by the young husband's family; in which case, it is more than probable, his career might have been very different. As it was, however, his mother and his father's trustees, Lord Dorchester, Lord Carlisle, and Nicholas Lechmere, thought it advisable temporarily to separate man and wife, and sent the Marquis abroad in charge of a French Protestant.

In this uncongenial company Philip visited Holland and Hanover and other German courts, and eventually settled down at Geneva. There he remained for a while, galled by the restrictions upon his personal liberty by the tutor, and infuriated by the inadequacy of the income allowed him by his trustees. The latter annoyance he overcame by raising money at, of course, exorbitant interest; the former by the simple expedient of running away from Geneva without his companion, who, a few hours after the flight of his charge, received from the latter a note: "Being no longer able to bear your ill-usage, I have thought proper to be gone from you; however, that you may not want company, I have left you the bear, as the most suitable companion in the world that could be picked out for you!"

Philip, Duke of Wharton

The Marquis made his way to Lyons, where he arrived on 13th October 1716, and from there he sent a complimentary letter to the son of James II. at Avignon, and with the letter, as a present, a magnificent horse. The Pretender, delighted by the prospect of being able to detach from the Hanoverian interest even an eighteen-year-old marquis, and especially the son of that very pronounced Whig, Thomas Wharton, graciously despatched one of his Court to invite Philip to Avignon. There the lad went, stayed a day and night, and received from his host the dangerous compliment of an offer of the title of the Duke of Northumberland, after which, to make matters worse, he repaired to St Germain's to pay his respects to Mary, Queen Dowager of England. The folly of his actions is the most remarkable thing about them. Had he been attached to the cause of the Chevalier de St George, the visits would have been natural; had he even desired, as so many had done, to be sufficiently attentive to the Prince so as to be free from molestation in case the latter should ever ascend the throne of England, the visits would have been explicable; but since he was not a Jacobite, and, if not too honest, at least too careless of his personal interest to be a "trimmer," the only solution of the matter is that his actions were dictated by a spirit of revolt, the not unnatural reaction on escaping from custody.

How little the Marquis meant by his visits—which, in after days, he declared were mere personal courtesies—may be deduced from the fact that, as soon as he arrived at Paris, he called on Lord Stair, the English Ambassador—at whose table, it is said, in a drunken frolic he proposed the health of the Pretender! At a time when it was a matter of vital importance to know who was for and against the home Government, and when a fortune was spent on spies, Lord Stair, of course, knew that the Marquis had been to Avignon and St Germain's; but if he did not close his ears to the tales of the young man's doings, at least he did not avert his countenance from him. On the contrary, he received him with every attention, realising that here was, so to speak, a brand to be plucked from the burning. The lad was only eighteen, and so indiscretions might be dismissed as of no importance; whereas to dwell on them unduly would perhaps turn him into a Jacobite. Therefore much show of kindness was diplomatic, coupled, Lord Stair thought, with a trifle of admonition.

However, when the Ambassador began to utter a word in season, the Marquis did not show himself amenable to advice. Indeed, when Lord Stair, extolling the virtues of his guest's father, said, "I hope you will follow so illustrious an example of fidelity to your Prince and love to your country," the Marquis retorted, "I thank your Excellency for your good counsel, and as your Excellency had also a worthy and deserving father, I hope that you will likewise copy so bright an original and tread in all his steps"—which reply, though showing a keen sense of humour, was brutal, for the first Lord Stair had unhesitatingly betrayed his sovereign!

As a matter of fact, the Marquis would tolerate no interference, and when a friend, whether or not set to task by Lord Stair has not transpired, expostulated with him for having abandoned the principles of his father, "I have pawned my principles," he said jauntily, "to Gordon, the Pretender's banker, for a considerable sum; and till I have the money to repay him, I must be a Jacobite; but," he added, "as soon as I have redeemed them, I shall be a Whig again!"

Perhaps this remark was conveyed to the Marquis's trustees, for it is to be presumed that the Marquis's financial obligations were discharged, since on his arrival in Ireland at the beginning of 1717 the Government seems to have connived at his taking his seat as Marquis Castlereagh, in the Irish House of Lords, though only in his nineteenth year—"which," Budgell wrote to Mr Secretary Addison, "is the highest compliment that could have been paid to him." Here Philip showed an apparently earnest desire to atone for his misdemeanours abroad, and his great talents made the task easy. He took a prominent part in debate, sat on committees, and in his official capacity conducted himself so that the British Government, congratulating themselves on their tact in having made light of his doings in France, thought it well to endeavour to bend him still more closely to their interests, by bestowing on him, perhaps as a set-off against the ducal title offered by the Pretender, an English dukedom.

"As it is the honour of subjects, who are descended from an illustrious family, to imitate the great examples of their ancestors, we esteem it no less our glory, as a King, after the manner of our predecessors, to dignify eminent methods by suitable rewards," so ran the preamble to the patent. "It is on this account that we confer a new title on our right trusty and entirely beloved cousin, Philip Marquis of Wharton and Malmesbury, who though he be born of a very ancient noble family, wherein he may reckon as many patriots as forefathers, has rather chosen to distinguish himself by his personal merit. The British nation, not forgetful of his father lately deceased, gratefully remember how much their invincible King William III. owed to that constant and courageous assistor of the public liberty and the Protestant religion. The same extraordinary person deserved so well of us, in having supported our interests by the weight of his councils, the force of his wit, and the firmness of his mind, at a time when our title to the succession of this realm was endangered; that in the beginning of our reign we invested him with the dignity of a Marquis, as an earnest of our royal favour, the farther marks whereof we were prevented from bestowing by his death, too hasty, and untimely for his King and Country. When we see the son of that great man, forming himself by so worthy an example, and in every action exhibiting a lively resemblance to his father; when we consider the eloquence which he has exerted with so much applause in the parliament of Ireland; and his turn and application, even in early youth, to the serious and weighty affairs of the public, we willingly decree him honours, which are neither superior to his merits, nor earlier than the expectation of our good subjects."

Vanity, it is generally assumed, was the moving spirit of the new Duke of Wharton, and it seems that to have earned a dukedom at twenty years of age temporarily lulled that passion, for, after the bestowal of that high honour, the recipient seems to have rested on his oars, and for the next year to have abandoned himself to unbridled excesses in drink and profligacy. "Aye, my lord," said Swift, who admired his talents, when his Grace had been recounting some of his frolics to the Dean of St Patrick's, "Aye, my lord, you have had many frolics; but let me recommend you one more: take a frolic to be virtuous; I assure you it will do you more honour than all the rest!"

Whether caused by Swift's words, or whether it was the swing of the pendulum, on coming of age Philip made a complete change in his mode of living, and for a while led a decent private life. "The Duke of Wharton has brought his Duchess to town, and is fond of her to distraction; to break the hearts of all the other women that have any claim on his," Lady Mary Wortley Montagu wrote to her sister, Lady Mar. "He has public devotions twice a day, and assists at them in person with exemplary devotion; and there is nothing pleasanter than the remarks of some great pious ladies on the conversion of so great a sinner." How long this period of conjugal fidelity might have endured is uncertain, but it was brought to an untimely end when the Duchess, in defiance of her husband's command, came from Winchendon to London, bringing with her their child, the twelve-months' old Earl of Malmesbury, who in the metropolis caught smallpox and died.

This, it is said by all loyal biographers, so affected his Grace that, regarding the bereavement as caused by the violation of his wishes, he could not bear the sight of his wife. Persons less prone to sentiment than biographers may perhaps see in this yet another swing of the pendulum.

If the Duke's private life was for a while exemplary, the same cannot at any time be said of his political career. A young man may change his opinion once without giving serious offence, he may even be forgiven for reverting to his earlier beliefs, but he can expect but scant mercy if he chops and changes with every breath of wind. At Avignon Philip had accepted a title from the Pretender, in Ireland he had accepted a dukedom from George I. as a reward for his vigorous support of the ministry; but now, when he took his seat in the English Parliament, to the general astonishment, he threw himself into uncompromising opposition.

The report of his great talents, his brilliant oratory, and his powers as a debater had reached Westminster, where his appearance was eagerly awaited, and he felt it incumbent upon him to show that rumour had not magnified his gifts; on 24th April 1720 he took part in a debate on a Bill to give further powers to the South Sea Company, and made a magnificent onslaught not only on this proposal, but on the entire policy of the Government, concluding with a terrible attack on Lord Stanhope, whom he accused of having made, or at least of having fostered, the breach between the King and the Prince of Wales, comparing him to Sejanus, "that evil and too powerful minister who made a division in the Imperial party, and rendered the reign of Tiberius hateful to the Romans." Lord Stanhope was not the man to sit quiet under such castigation, and he turned the tables on his assailant with undoubted dexterity. "The Romans were most certainly a great people, and furnished many illustrious examples in their history, which ought to be carefully read," he said in reply. "The Romans were likewise universally allowed to be a wise people, and they showed themselves to be so in nothing more than by debarring young noblemen from speaking in the Senate till they understood good manners and propriety of language; and as the Duke has quoted an instance from this history of a bad minister, I beg leave to quote from the same history an instance of a great man, a patriot of his country, who had a son so profligate that he would have betrayed the liberties of it, on which account his father himself had him whipped to death."

The Minister's apt retort rankled, and it doubtless did much to confirm the Duke in his attitude. He spoke against the Government, not only in the House of Lords, but in the City of London and in the country; and in the following year, returning to the question of the South Sea Company's affairs, he attacked Lord Stanhope in so brilliant and bitter a speech that the latter, rising in a passion to reply, broke a blood-vessel, from the effects of which he died on the following day. It was somewhat later that the Duke attacked Lord Chancellor Macclesfield, suspected and eventually found guilty of fraud in connection with the South Sea Company's affairs, not only by word of mouth, but also in a satirical ballad entitled "An Epistle from John Sheppard to the Earl of Macclesfield":

"Were thy virtues and mine to be weighed in a scale,

I fear, honest Thomas, that thine would prevail,

For you break through all laws, while I only break jail.

Which nobody can deny.

When curiosity led you so far

As to send for me, my dear lord, to the bar,

To show what a couple of rascals we were.

Which nobody can deny.

You'll excuse me the freedom of writing to thee,

For all the world then agreed they never did see

A pair so well matched as your lordship and me.

Which nobody can deny.

At the present disgrace, my lord! ne'er repine,

Since fame thinks of nothing but thy tricks and mine,

And our name shall alike in history shine.

Which nobody can deny."

Having established his fame as an orator with his speeches on the South Sea question, Wharton gained yet further distinction by his impassioned defence of Bishop Atterbury, but what reputation he gained as a speaker he lost in honour, for he had obtained the material for his oration by a mean trick. The day before he spoke he went to Sir Robert Walpole, told him he was sorry for his opposition to the Government and intended to reinstate himself in favour at Court and with the Ministry by speaking against the Bishop, and he begged the Prime Minister to give him some assistance in preparing his arguments. Walpole went carefully over the ground with his visitor, and showed him the strong and the weak points of the case. The Duke expressed his thanks, spent the night in a drinking bout, and, without going to bed, went to the House of Lords and spoke *for* the Bishop, making use most effectively of the information he had obtained on the previous day. Then, when sentence of banishment was pronounced on the Bishop, he saw him off, and, returning home, wrote and published some verses on "The Banishment of Cicero," in which, of course, the Bishop was Cicero, and George I. Clodius, concluding:

"Let Clodius now in grandeur reign,

Let him exert his power,

A short-lived monster in the land,

The monarch of an hour;

Let pageant fools adore their wooden god,

And act against their senses at his nod.

Pierced by an untimely hand

To earth shall he descend,

Though now with gaudy honours clothed,

Inglorious in his end.

Blest be the man who does his power defy,

And dares, or truly speaks, or bravely die!"

In the meantime the Duke had reverted to his dissipated habits in private life, and it amused and annoyed many of his contemporaries that in public he, the President of the Hell-fire Club, should, on the ground of morality, inveigh against various measures. Wharton, however, paid little or no heed to those who held the view that a profligate is not the proper person to preach virtue; but when the King in council, on 29th April 1721, issued a proclamation against "certain scandalous clubs or society, who in the most impious and blasphemous manner insult the most sacred principles of our holy religion, and corrupt the minds and morals of one another," Wharton, as President of the Hell-fire Club, rose in his place in the House of Lords, declared he was not, as was thought, a "patron of blasphemy," and, pulling out a Bible, proceeded to read several texts.

He went occasionally to his seat in Westmoreland, and was a frequent visitor to the seat of his kinsman, Sir Christopher Musgrave, at Edenhall, where was preserved the great crystal goblet, supposed to have been seized by some earlier Musgrave from a fairy banquet, and known as "The Luck of Edenhall." The legend ran:

"If this glass do break or fall,
Farewell the luck of Edenhall!"

but in spite of this warning the Duke, out of sheer devilment, would toss the goblet high in the air, and once, but for a wary butler, it would have fallen to the ground and have been smashed to atoms. It was at Edenhall that the Homeric drinking match took place, which Wharton, its proposer, celebrated in verse in the form of "An Imitation of Chevvy-Chace."

"God prosper long our noble king,

And likewise *Eden-Hall*;

A doleful Drinking-Bout I sing,

There lately did befal.

To chace the Spleen with Cup and Can

Duke *Philip* took his Way;

Babes yet unborn shall never see

Such Drinking as that Day.

The stout and ever thirsty Duke

A vow to God did make

His pleasure within *Cumberland*

Three live-long Nights to take.

Sir *Musgrave* too of Martindale,

A true and worthy knight,

Eftsoons with him a Bargain made

In drinking to delight.

The Bumper swiftly pass'd about,

Six in a Hand went round,

And with their Calling for more Wine,

They made the Hall resound."

So began the ballad, and it goes on to tell how the news of the battle spread, how others then hastened to the board, and fell, man by man, overcome by their potations.

The Duke, however, did not care for his place in the north, and was more frequently to be found at Twickenham, a fact duly noted by Horace Walpole in his "Parish Register" of that village:

"Twickenham, where frolic Wharton revelled,

Where Montagu, with locks dishevelled,

Conflict of dirt and warmth combin'd,

Invoked,—and scandalised the *Nine*."

It was not by accident that Walpole put these names in juxtaposition, for there was a great intimacy between the two, and it was said, probably with reason, that it was the Duke's attentions to the lady that turned Pope's affection to hatred and caused the historic breach between them. But though Lady Mary "Worldly" Montagu, as Philip called her, may have been attached to the Duke, she was never in any doubt as to the worthlessness of his professions of love. "In general, gallantry never was in so elevated a figure as it is at present," she told Lady Mar. "Twenty very pretty fellows (the Duke of Wharton being president and chief director) have formed themselves into a committee of gallantry. They call themselves *Schemers*; and meet regularly three times a week, to consult on gallant schemes for the advantage and advancement of that branch of happiness."

Wharton's gallantries, or, to give them their proper though less euphonious name, profligacies, were carried to such excess that they, together with his political infidelities, disgusted even his far from strait-laced contemporaries; and it was only his great talents that enabled him to hold his own with them. But his marvellous gift of oratory and his ingenious but always sound reasoning were appreciated even by, or, perhaps, it should be said, especially by, his enemies; while his occasional outbursts of humour made it difficult for anyone to keep a straight face. Who could help laughing when a certain Bishop in the House of Lords rose to speak and remarked he should divide what he had to say into twelve parts, and Wharton, interrupting, begged he might be permitted to tell a story that could only be introduced at that moment: "A drunken fellow was passing by St Paul's at night, and heard the clock slowly chiming twelve. He counted the strokes, and when it was finished, looking towards the clock, said, 'Damn you, why couldn't you give us all that at once?' " There was an end of the Bishop's speech!

But not great talents, combined with a keen sense of humour, could save a person as volatile as the Duke. He founded in 1723 an Opposition paper, *The True Briton*, written by himself, issued twice weekly, which secured a large circulation, and for publishing which, Payne, indicted for libel, and found guilty, was heavily fined; but this may be regarded as a legitimate political move. As he was known to be in correspondence with the Pretender, it is not easy to see how he escaped impeachment, unless it was that the Government was reluctant to proceed against a young man, the son of a valued supporter and an old friend of Sir Robert Walpole, and the godson of the two preceding sovereigns of Great Britain.

The Government, however, was soon relieved from any anxiety on this score, for the Duke's extravagance in money matters had been so great that his creditors had, for their own benefit, obtained a decree of the Court of Chancery placing his estates in the hands of trustees until his liabilities had been liquidated. These trustees allowed his Grace an income of twelve hundred pounds, upon which, deciding it was impossible in this country to support his dignity on that sum, he left England, thus bringing to a close the first act of his wasted life.

Before the Duke went abroad he had been careful to make his peace with the Pretender, for the latter, writing in 1725 to Atterbury, then at Paris, says: "I am very glad you were to send into England . . . for everybody is not so active as Lord Wharton, who writes me often and wants no spur." The Pretender had not yet discovered the danger of a follower so wayward and unreliable as this young man, who did more harm than good to any cause he espoused; and so, when the Duke arrived on the Continent in May 1725, he sent him as envoy to Vienna to do his utmost to promote a good understanding between his master and the Emperor Charles VI. In this Wharton was not altogether unsuccessful, and when he reported the result of his mission the Chevalier de St George, then resident at Rome, rewarded him with the empty title of Duke of Northumberland and the Order of the Garter.

In the following April the Duke was sent to Madrid, where his folly became notorious. "The Duke of Wharton has not been sober, or scarce had a pipe out of his mouth, since he came back from his expedition to St Ildefonso," wrote Mr (afterwards Sir Benjamin) Keene, British Ambassador at Madrid. "He declared himself to be the Pretender's Prime Minister, and Duke of Wharton and Northumberland. Hitherto, added he, my master's interest has been managed by the Duke of Perth and three or four old women, who meet under the portal of St Germain's. He wanted a Whig, and a brisk one too, to put them in a right train, and I am the man. You may now look upon me, Sir Philip Wharton, knight of the Garter, and Sir Robert Walpole, knight of the Bath, running a course,—and, by heaven! he shall be pressed hard. He bought my family pictures, but they shall not be long in his possession; that account is still open." In spite of the Duke's follies, the Court of Spain did not show itself so unfriendly to him, and to the cause he represented, as Keene thought it should; and he warned his Government.

The reply from England came in the form of a summons under the Privy Seal to the Duke to return at once to his own country—a summons which, it is needless to say, was ignored by the recipient.

While at Madrid Philip learnt that his wife, whom he had left in London, had died, and forthwith he proposed to Maria, the daughter of Colonel Henry O'Beirne, a lady-in-waiting to the Queen of Spain. Her Majesty raised various objections, but was eventually persuaded to consent to the alliance, which took place in July 1726, after the Duke had embraced the Roman Catholic faith, a step he took in spite of the fact that on 17th June he had written to his sister, Lady Jane Holt, assuring her he would never forsake the religion in which he had been born and bred.

It is probable that the Duke changed his faith to win his bride, but there may have been at the back of his mind the thought that it would please his master. If this was so, it was an entirely mistaken idea, because his conversion—occurring at the same time as that of Lord North, who had also left England and abjured the Hanoverian cause—gave the impression that to be in favour with the Chevalier de St George it was necessary to be of his faith, which in English eyes was a fatal objection. This, indeed, the Chevalier had realised, as may be gathered from a letter of the Duchess of Orleans, so far back as 10th September 1712: "Our King of England, I mean the true one, no longer dislikes Protestants, for he has taken many of them for his servants." What Atterbury thought of the Duke's action, he said very clearly in a letter to the Pretender: "The strange turn taken by the Duke of Wharton gave me such mortifying apprehensions that I have forborne for some posts to mention him at all. You say, Sir, that he advised with few of his friends in this matter. I am of opinion he advised with none. It is easy to suppose you were both surprised and concerned at the account when it first reached Rome, since it is impossible you should not be so; the ill consequences are so many, so great, and so evident, that I am not only afflicted but bewildered when I think of them. The mischief of one thing you mention is, that he will scarce be believed in what he shall say in that occasion (so low will his credit have sunk), nor be able effectually to stop the mouth of malice by any after declaration." In England nothing that the Duke of Wharton could do created any astonishment, such was the estimate in which he was held in his own country; and popular opinion was expressed by Curll in an epigram:

On the Duke of Wharton Renouncing the Protestant Religion

"A *Whig* He was bred, but at length is turn'd *Papist*,

Pray God send the next Remove be not an *Atheist*.

"N.B.—To believe *every Thing* and *Nothing* is much the same."

After his marriage, the Duke paid a visit to his master at Rome, but he "could not keep himself within the bounds of the Italian gravity," and the Chevalier ordered him and his wife to return to Spain. There he volunteered to serve with the Spanish army in the siege of Gibraltar. Hitherto there had been some suspicion of his courage, but that slur he now wiped off by exposing his person freely; indeed, the story goes that one day he walked from the Spanish camp to the very walls of Gibraltar, and, when challenged, declared his identity, and sauntered back leisurely, the soldiers, unwilling to kill a great nobleman of their own nationality, holding their fire.

After the siege, the Duke returned to Madrid, where he was given the rank of Colonel-Aggregate to the Irish regiment, Hibernia, in the Spanish service, commanded by the Marquis de Castelar; and then proposed to settle for a while at the Pretender's Court. That royal personage, however, had by this time realised that his adherent's gifts were so handicapped by various undesirable qualities that he showed very plainly that he wished any intimate connection should cease: he did, indeed, consent to grant a last interview at Parma, but he neutralised the effect of this favour by taking the opportunity to refuse to allow the Duke to reside at his Court.

The Duke took the rebuff in good part, wrote to the Chevalier reiterating his great and enduring devotion to the Jacobite cause, and, journeying with his wife to Paris, in that city at once made overtures to Horace Walpole, the British Ambassador. "I am coming to Paris, to put myself entirely under your Excellency's protection, and hope that Sir Robert Walpole's good nature will prompt him to save a family, which his generosity induced him to spare," he wrote in May 1728. "If your Excellency would permit me to wait upon you for an hour, I am certain you would be convinced of the sincerity of my repentance for my former madness; would become an advocate with his Majesty to grant me his most gracious pardon, which it is my comfort I shall never be required to purchase by any step unworthy of a man of honour. I do not intend, in the case of the king's allowing me to pass the evening of my days under the shadow of his royal protection, to see England for some years, but shall remain in France or Germany, as my friends shall advise, and enjoy country sports till all former stories are buried in oblivion. I beg of your Excellency to let me receive your orders at Paris, which I will send to your hotel to receive. The Duchess of Wharton, who is with me, desires leave to wait on Mrs Walpole, if you think proper."

Horace Walpole received him, listened to his assurances of future loyalty, and conveyed his protestations of good behaviour to the Duke of Newcastle, who replied on 12th July:

"Having laid before the King your Excellency's letter, giving an account of a visit you had received from the Duke of Wharton, and enclosing a copy of a letter he wrote to you afterwards upon the same occasion, I am commanded to let you know that his Majesty approves of what you said to the Duke, and your behaviour towards him; but that the Duke of Wharton has conducted himself in so extraordinary a manner since he left England, and has so openly declared his disaffection to the King and his government, by joining with and serving under his Majesty's professed enemies, that his Majesty does not think fit to receive any application from him."

It is unnecessary to give in detail the subsequent actions of the Duke: how, incensed by the King's refusal, he printed in *Mist's Journal* a bitter satirical attack on George II. and his ministers; how he was tried for high treason for having taken up arms against his country, found guilty, outlawed, and deprived of his property; how at the eleventh hour unofficial overtures were made to him from England, which he refused to entertain unless unconditional pardon was granted him; how he stayed awhile in a monastery, a fervent devotee, and after a few weeks returned to the world to plunge into greater excesses; how he publicly proclaimed his attachment to the Pretender and the Catholic religion.

His estates being sequestrated, he was now penniless, and reduced to most miserable straits. "Notwithstanding what my Brother Madman has done to undo himself, and everybody who was so unlucky as to have the least concern with him," wrote a friend who journeyed with him from Paris to Orleans at the beginning of June 1729, "I could not help being sensibly moved at so extraordinary a vicissitude of fortune, to see a great man fallen from that shining light, in which I have beheld him in the House of Lords, to such a degree of obscurity, that I have observed the meanest commoner decline his company; and the Jew he would sometimes fasten on, grow tired of it; for you know he is but a bad orator in his cups, and of late he has been but seldom sober." Eventually, after overcoming great difficulties, the Duke arrived in Spain, where he joined his regiment, and endeavoured to live upon his pay of eighteen pistoles a month, and sums of money sent to him by the Pretender. He devoted his leisure to reading and to the composition of a play based on the tragic story of Mary Queen of Scots, and, after an illness of some months, he died on 31st May 1731, at the age of thirty-two, in the shelter of the Franciscan monastery of Poblet.

Such is the story of the life of Philip, Duke of Wharton, which, surely, arouses feelings of pity rather than anger. "Like Buckingham and Rochester," says Horace Walpole, "he comforted all the grave and dull by throwing away the brightest profusion of parts on witty fooleries, debaucheries, and scrapes, which may mix graces with a great character, but can never compose one." He had, indeed, genius, wit, humour, eloquence, rank, wealth and good looks, but because he lacked stability and principles, all his great talents went for nothing. Never was there a character more fitted to point a moral, and if the writers of Sunday school prize-books have not taken him as their text, this can only be because they are unacquainted with his history. "The great abilities of the Duke of Wharton are past dispute," Atterbury wrote to the Pretender, in September 1736; "it is he alone who could render them less useful than they might have been." And this was kindly put, for Atterbury might well have said that as an adherent to any cause so unreliable and faithless a person was an open danger.

For every man some excuse can be found, but while excuses for the Duke of Wharton there must be, it is, indeed, not easy to find them. His early training may have been unsuitable for a character so mercurial, and the early death of his mother and father probably removed any change of controlling him. That he was mad is a theory practical enough, for this would explain many sudden changes of opinion, and many instances of unfaithfulness, which had not even self-interest to explain them; and it seems certain that he was intoxicated with vanity. This last assumption is supported by the testimony of Pope, who has for all time put on record a character sketch of the Duke, which, in spite of the poet's bias, must unfortunately be accepted as a portrait all too true:

"Wharton, the scorn and wonder of our days,

Whose ruling passion was the lust of praise:

Born with whate'er could win it from the wise,

Women and fools must like him or he dies;

Though wondering senates hung on all he spoke,

The club must hail him master of the joke.

Shall parts so various aim at nothing new?

He'll shine a Tully and a Wilmot too,

Then turn repentant, and his God adores

With the same spirit that he drinks and w——;

Enough if all around him but admire,

And now the punk applaud, and now the friar.

Thus with each gift of nature and of art,

And wanting nothing but an honest heart;

Grown all to all, from no one vice exempt;

And most contemptible, to shun contempt:

His passion still, to covet general praise,

His life, to forfeit it a thousand ways;

A constant bounty which no friend has made;

An angel tongue, which no man can persuade;

A fool, with more of wit than half mankind,

Too rash for thought, for action too refined:

A tyrant to the wife his heart approves;

A rebel to the very king he loves;

He dies, sad outcast of each church and state,

And, harder still, flagitious, yet not great.

Ask you why Wharton broke through every rule?

'Twas all for fear the knaves should call him fool."

FOOTNOTES:

1 Barouches were so described on their first introduction into England.

2 "Life, Adventures, and Opinions of Colonel George Hanger."

3 Hanger wrote a pamphlet on rat-catching.

4 Dibdin's *Mother Goose*, which ran for a hundred nights at Covent Garden.

5 Sir Pepper Arden was a man of very violent temperament. One day, when he was haranguing a jury, a Frenchman who was paying a visit to the Law Courts asked who was the irascible advocate. His companion translated the name literally, "*Le Chevalier Poivre Ardent.*" "*Parbleu!*" replied the other, "*il est très bien nommé.*"

6 At a grand review at Brighton he was thrown from his horse and broke his classical Roman nose.

7 A visitor to Brummell met the great man's valet on the stair having on his arm a number of crumpled ties. In answer to an inquiring look, the latter explained, "They are our failures."

8 The Duke of Bedford asked his opinion of a new coat; Brummell looked at it carefully in front and, telling him to turn round, at the back. Then he asked earnestly, "Bedford, do you call this thing a coat?"

9 Hoby died worth one hundred and twenty thousand pounds. He was the first man in London to drive a Tilbury.

10 Drummond was a partner in the great banking-house of that name, and the episode caused his retirement from the firm. This was the only occasion on which he had played whist at White's Club.

11 Solomon was a well-known money-lender.

12 Brummell still interested himself in fashion. He wrote in 1818 from Calais to Raikes: "I heard of you the other day in a waistcoat that does you indisputable credit, spick and span from Paris, a broad stripe, salmon colour and cramoisi. Keep it up, my dear fellow, and don't let them laugh you into a relapse so Gothic as that of your former English simplicity."

13 It was said Sir Thomas Rumbold was originally a waiter at White's, obtained an appointment in India, and rose to be Governor of Madras. This, however, has been demonstrated to be merely a legend by his descendant, Sir Horace Rumbold.

-14 Born 1724; succeeded to the Earldom of March, 1731, and, on his mother's death, to the Earldom of Ruglen; inherited the dukedom, 1778; died 23rd December 1810.

15 The Bank of England.

16 From Alderman Richard Sclater is descended the present Lord Basing, by whose generous courtesy the present writer has had access to the unpublished letters, preserved at Hoddington House, written from India by Elizabeth Sclater, afterwards Mrs Draper, to members of her family in England. Passages from these letters are printed in this article.

17 British Museum, Add. MSS. 34527.

18 *Bombay Quarterly Review*, January 1857, p. 191. The article is anonymous, and can scarcely have been written by one who knew Mrs Draper, though he may well have been acquainted with those who had.

19 British Museum, Add. MSS. 34527.

20 It has hitherto been assumed that "Don Pringello" was the playful form given by the Demoniacs to one Pringle. The present writer has been so fortunate as to enlist the kind offices of Mr W. J. Locke and Mr Rudolf Dircks in an endeavour to trace this architect; but neither an English Pringle nor a Spanish Don Pringello has been discovered.

Milton Keynes UK
Ingram Content Group UK Ltd.
UKHW011143220424
441551UK00007B/780